DO
YOU
HAVE
AN EXIT
STRATEGY?

DO
YOU
HAVE
AN EXIT
STRATEGY?

Mary Detweiler

Published in the United States of America by Credo House Publishers, a division of Credo Communications, LLC, Grand Rapids, Michigan
credohousepublishers.com

ISBN: 978-1-62586-200-6

Cover design by Valerie Feller
Interior design by Frank Gutbrod
Editing by Donna Huisjen

Printed in the United States of America

First edition

To individuals in the final season of their life. I wrote these words for you. I hope that as you read my words and the words of others you will realize that when your physical body dies, *you* still exist. Further, you have the power to choose *where* you will exist.

Table of Contents

INTRODUCTION

For everything there is a season,
a time for every activity under heaven.
A time to be born and a time to die.
(Ecclesiastes 3:1–2)

No one is going to get out of this life alive. No matter how much we may prefer not to think about this, it is an undeniable truth. Since death is inevitable, it is wise to plan for it.

By planning for it, I am not talking about preparing a will, designating powers of attorney to make decisions for you when you are no longer able to do so, filling out medical advance directives, leaving enough money for your loved ones to pay your final expenses, and so forth. Though these are good and important things, I am talking about having an exit strategy for what will happen to *you* when your body dies.

When that happens, you will be released from your body's physical bonds into eternity. You have no choice about this. You do, however, have a choice as to where you will spend eternity. Your home for eternity is entirely in your control. It will be determined based on where you're at with God when you die.

Now, I know that some of you reading these words already disagree with me. You don't believe in God, you don't believe there is more to us than our physical bodies, and you don't believe in an afterlife. If this is you, I urge you to hang in there with me and read this. It is written for you.

Some of you reading this book do believe in God and do believe in an afterlife; however, you either don't know where you're at with God or don't understand what I mean by that. If this is you, the first two chapters may not be necessary for you to read (unless you want to, of course). You can begin at chapter three. The rest of the chapters will pertain to you, and I encourage you to read them carefully and thoughtfully.

Finally, since I have never *not* believed God existed, I find it difficult to communicate with agnostics and atheists in a way that may open their hearts to believe in him. Therefore, I leaned very heavily on the words and experiences of others in the first two chapters.

Since I believed in God's existence long before I had a relationship with him, the remainder of the book consists primarily of my own words, as well as my own experiences and struggles to enter into a relationship with him. I am sharing my story in the hope that my experiences and struggles will resonate with some of you and will encourage you to take the leap of faith to put your life in God's hands.

They are the only hands, in my opinion, that will hold you safely and lovingly in this life and in the life to come. I hope this becomes your exit strategy.

CHAPTER ONE

INESCAPABLE QUESTIONS

If you are reading this, you may very well be facing the end of your life, and questions that you have either not thought about or intentionally ignored are now front and center in your mind. Questions such as:

- What happens when I die?
- Is God real?
- Is there an afterlife?
- If there is an afterlife, what is it like?

I am going to address each of these questions in a way that I hope you will find, at the very least, informative. Before I jump into the meat of this, though, I want to lay the following groundwork: it is important to emphasize that I am *not* trying to convert you to a religion. I am going to ask you to carefully consider some evidence I will present of God's existence, and I am going to ask you to reflect on what is stopping you from believing God exists.

The first question—What happens when I die?—was addressed in the introduction. To reiterate, when your body dies, you are released from its physical bonds into eternity. You have no choice about this. You do, however, have a choice as to where you will spend eternity. Your home for eternity is entirely in your control. It will be determined based on where you're at with God when you die.

This leads right into the second question: Is God real? If you're reading this, I am assuming you have decided, or at least considered the possibility, that God is not real. If this is the case, what led you to *not* believe in God?

As I was doing research for this book, I came across various reasons people choose agnosticism (a noncommittal stance) or atheism. Some of these reasons are:

- It seemed like the most logical, rational choice.
- You were taught as a child that there is no God.
- You experienced negative, hurtful, and/or traumatic childhood experiences in religious institutions or in relationships with clergy, parents, or other adults.
- You chose skepticism or atheism because of the evil and suffering you saw in the world.
- You chose skepticism or atheism because you can't wrap your mind around a God who sends good people to hell.
- Science seemed to explain the world and life.

Though I am sure this is not an exhaustive list of reasons for avoiding the issue or choosing atheism, they seem to be some of the most prominent. I will address each one in turn.

The rational road

Author Ernest Hemingway chose atheism because it seemed to be the most logical, rational choice. In his book *A Farewell to Arms*, Hemingway stated, "All thinking men are atheists."[1] In my opinion, *some* thinking men and women are atheists, some are noncommittal on the issue, and *some* thinking men and women are believers.

God gave most of us a working intellect. Of those who choose to use their intellect to investigate whether or not God exists, some reach the conclusion that he does not exist (atheists), some insist that we have no way of determining this one way or the other (agnostics), and some reach the conclusion that he is alive and well on planet Earth (believers).

Contrary to popular belief, rational thought and belief in God are not necessarily at odds. In his book *The Reason for God*, Timothy Keller advocates for a belief in God that is grounded in sound reasoning.

> People who blithely go through life too busy or indifferent to ask hard questions about why they believe as they do will find themselves defenseless against either the experience of tragedy or the probing questions of a smart skeptic. . . . Believers should acknowledge and wrestle with doubts. . . . All doubts, however skeptical and cynical they may seem, are really a set of alternate beliefs. You

cannot doubt Belief A except from a position of faith in Belief B. . . . Every doubt, therefore, is based on a leap of faith.[2]

Josh McDowell and Sean McDowell advocate for the same thing in their book *Evidence That Demands a Verdict*. "Faith is meant to go along with evidence, not run contrary to it."[3]

Inherited belief

To those of you who were taught as a child that there is no God, I encourage you to take an honest look at whether you freely chose atheism or whether you fell into it without any conscious consideration.

As one moves into adulthood, it is important to establish a firm foundation upon which to live one's adult life. Part of establishing that foundation is making decisions about one's values and beliefs. One can either choose to adopt parents' and/or culture's values and beliefs and live one's life accordingly, one can avoid the issue altogether, or one can choose a different set of values and beliefs. The operative word here is *choose*.

If a young adult makes choices regarding values and beliefs to either please or spite parents, the parents' values and beliefs are the starting point. The individual is reacting to something external, the parents' values and beliefs, rather than responding to something internal, the beginning formation of their adult self. If a young adult does make these decisions with parental values and beliefs as the starting point, however, all is not lost. One can do the emotional work necessary at any point in their adult life to establish oneself as an independent adult separate from parents and implement a course correction. Again, the operative word here is *choose*.

Important note: The separation I am talking about here is an emotional separation, not a physical one. It has nothing to do with geography. It has to do with choices.

Keller states, "It is no longer sufficient to hold beliefs just because you inherited them. Only if you struggle long and hard with objections to your faith will you be able to provide grounds for your beliefs."[4]

Hurt into it

To those of you who chose atheism because of childhood experiences you had in religious institutions or in relationships with clergy, parents, or other adults, I am truly sorry this happened to you. The only thing I can say to you is that it was human beings who hurt you, maybe even traumatized you. God did not hurt you. Josh McDowell provides us with a clear and heartbreaking example of this:

> My ultimate problem wasn't intellectual—it was emotional. I had bitterness and hatred for my father because he was an alcoholic and destroyed my family. In addition, the sexual abuse I experienced for seven years by Wayne Bailey [a worker on his family's farm] just compounded the hurt. Given my father's failures, it brought me no joy to hear that a heavenly Father supposedly loved me. Every time someone mentioned a

"heavenly Father," it didn't bring joy—it brought pain. I could not decipher the difference between a heavenly Father and an earthly father because in my world and in my experience, fathers hurt people. So I wanted nothing to do with God.[5]

I'm guessing that some of you might be thinking, *Okay, it was human beings who hurt me—but why did God let it happen?* My response to this is that he didn't *let* this happen. It happened because he gave each of us free will and because people are broken. God will not pick and choose whom he allows to exercise free will and whom he refuses to allow to exercise free will. If he takes free will away from one person, his consistent nature demands that he take it away from all of us. Would you like that? Would you like to lose your ability and power to make choices? I'm guessing not.

Regarding the brokenness of people, have you ever gone ahead and done something you didn't really want to do because you knew it was wrong or not good for you? That is evidence that there is something broken inside you. Enough said.

Woody Allen provides us with another example of how a negative experience can lead one to choose atheism. "I was raised in a religious home. It was unreasonable enforced religion that turned me off to it. It was a joyless, unpleasant, stupid, barbaric thing when I was a child and I've never gotten over that feeling."[6]

Evil and suffering

To those of you who chose atheism because of the evil and suffering you saw in the world, you are far from alone. According to Josh and Sean McDowell, "Evil and suffering become perhaps the most powerful reasons people struggle with the idea of God."[7] In their view, however,

> Evil is a departure from the way things ought to be, a corruption of good. Just as rust cannot exist without iron, and a lie cannot exist without truth, so evil steals and corrupts from good. This means that there can be good without evil, but not evil without good. . . . Ironically, then, when someone raises the problem of evil, that person is assuming there is such a thing as objective good. And if there is objective good, then there must be a God.
>
> C.S. Lewis was once an atheist who believed that evil disproved God. But upon deeper reflection, he changed his mind: "My argument against God was that the universe seemed so cruel and unjust. But how had I got this idea of *just* and *unjust*? A man does not call a line crooked unless he has some idea of a straight line. What was I comparing the universe with when I called it unjust?[8]

This raises the question of why God allows evil and suffering to exist in the world if he is a God of goodness. This brings us back to the concept of free will, though on a much broader scale. My response: While God *allows* evil and suffering to exist in the world, based on human choice, he never authors or instigates it; it exists because some people choose to use their free will to do evil rather than good, thereby causing others to suffer.

Hell? Really?

The next reason for choosing atheism, inability to wrap your mind around the concept of how a God of love can send people to hell, seems to flow almost naturally from the previous one. Keller addresses this one at length:

> God is both a God of love and of justice.[9] ... The Biblical picture is that sin separates us from the presence of God, which is the source of all joy and indeed of all love, wisdom, or good things of any sort. Since we were originally created for God's immediate presence, only before his face will we thrive, flourish, and achieve our highest potential. If we were to lose his presence totally, that would be hell—the loss of our capability for giving or receiving love or joy. A common image of hell in the Bible is that of fire. Fire disintegrates. Even in this life we can see the kind of soul disintegration that self-centeredness creates. We know how selfishness and self-absorption leads to piercing bitterness, nauseating envy, paralyzing anxiety, paranoid thoughts, and the mental denials and distortions that accompany them. Now ask the question: "What if when we die we don't end, but spiritually our life extends on into eternity?" Hell, then, is the trajectory of

a soul, living a self-absorbed, self-centered life, going on and on forever.[10] . . . All God does in the end with people is give them what they most want, including freedom from himself.[11]

Donald Carson, professor at Trinity Evangelical Divinity School, stated in an interview with Lee Strobel:

Hell is not a place where people are consigned because they were pretty good blokes but just didn't believe the right stuff. They're consigned there, first and foremost, because they defy their Maker and want to be at the center of the universe. . . . It's filled with people who, for all eternity, still want to be at the center of the universe and who persist in their God-defying rebellion.[12]

Keller also shared some of his own spiritual journey:

During my college years and my early twenties I, like so many others, questioned the Christian faith I was raised in. . . . I was troubled by those Christians who stressed hellfire and damnation. Like so many of my generation I believed that, if there was a core to all religions, it was a loving God. I wanted to believe in a God of love who accepted people regardless of their beliefs and practices . . . The source of the idea that God is Love is the Bible itself. And the Bible tells us that the God of love is also a God of judgment who will put all things in the world to rights in the end. The belief in a God of pure love—who accepts everyone and judges no one—is a powerful act of faith. Not only is there no evidence for it in the natural order, but there is almost no historical, religious textual support for it outside of Christianity. The more one looks at it, the less justified it appears.[13]

I look at it a bit differently, more simplistically. I consider heaven to be God's home. We are invited to share his home for eternity if we have a relationship with him. Now, I ask you, would you invite someone you did not have a relationship with to share your home forever? I wouldn't. I'm guessing you wouldn't either.

Science as theology

To those who chose atheism because science seemed to explain the world and life, meet Lee Strobel.

As a fourteen-year-old freshman at Prospect High School . . . I first heard the liberating information that propelled me toward a life of atheism. . . . I was incurably curious, always after answers, constantly trying to figure out how things worked. . . . I liked science. . . . Science gave me an excuse to ask all the "why" questions that plagued me, to try genetic experiments by breeding fruit flies, and to peer inside plants to learn about how they reproduced. . . . In Sunday school and confirmation classes during my junior high school years, my "why" questions weren't always welcomed . . . More often than not, my quest for answers was rebuffed.[14]

So the seeds of my atheism were sown as a youngster when religious authorities seemed unwilling or unable to help me get answers to my questions about God. My disbelief flowered after discovering that Darwinism displaces the need for a deity. And my atheism came to full bloom when I studied Jesus in college and was told that no science-minded person could possibly believe what the New Testament says about him.[15]

Strobel lived life content in his atheism until his wife became a believer in the autumn of 1979. As he watched his wife over time manifest "fundamental changes in her character, her integrity, and her personal confidence,"[16] he decided to put his atheism under a microscope and examine the evidence for his beliefs. "In my quest to determine if contemporary science points toward or away from God, I knew I had to first examine the claims of evolution in order to conclude once and for all whether Darwinism creates a reasonable foundation for atheism."[17] To that end Strobel interviewed the following experts in their respective fields:

- Jonathan Wells—molecular and cell biology
- Walter Bradley—origin of life
- Stephen C. Meyer—philosophy of science
- William Lane Craig—cosmology
- Robin Collins—physics and philosophy
- Guillermo Gonzalez—astronomy

CHAPTER TWO

A QUEST
FOR ANSWERS

Strobel began his quest by asking Jonathan Wells, molecular and cell biologist, to define Darwinian evolution, which he did: "Darwinism claims . . . that *all* living creatures are modified descendants of a common ancestor that lived long ago . . . that every new species that has ever appeared can be explained by descent with modification. Neo-Darwinism claims these modifications are the result of natural selection acting on random genetic mutations."[18]

When Strobel asked Wells about the images of evolution, considered to be the evidence for evolution, Wells stated that "much of what science teachers have been telling students is simply wrong."[19] Strobel and Wells then discussed each of the images at length and in depth. Some of the statements Wells made during the course of this discussion are:

- The problem of assembling the right parts in the right way at the right time and at the right place, while keeping out the wrong material, is simply insurmountable. Frankly, the idea that we're on the verge of explaining the origin of life naturalistically is just silly to me.[20]

- It's becoming clearer and clearer to me that this is materialistic philosophy masquerading as empirical science. The attitude is that life *had* to have developed this way because there's no other materialistic explanation. And if you try to invoke another explanation—for instance, intelligent design—then the evolutionists claim you're not a scientist.[21]

- As an illustration of the fossil record, the Tree of Life is a dismal failure. But it *is* a good representation of Darwin's theory. . . . Darwin knew the fossil record failed to support his tree. He acknowledged that major groups of animals—he calls them divisions, now they're called phyla—appear suddenly in the fossil record. That's not what his theory predicts. His theory predicts a long history of gradual divergence from a common ancestor, with the differences slowly becoming bigger and bigger until you get the major differences we have now. The fossil evidence, even in his day, showed the opposite: the rapid appearance of phylum-level differences in what's called the "Cambrian explosion." Darwin believed that future fossil discoveries would vindicate his theory—but that hasn't happened.[22]

- If you consider all of the evidence, Darwin's tree is false as a description of the history of life. I'll even go further than that: it's not even a good hypothesis at this point.[23]
- Lack of fossil evidence also makes it virtually impossible to reconstruct supposed relationships between ancestors and descendants.[24]
- Darwinists assume the story of human life is an evolutionary one, and then they plug the fossils into a preexisting narrative where they seem to fit. The narrative can take several forms depending on one's biases. As one anthropologist said, the process is "both political and subjective" to the point where he suggested that "paleoanthropology has the form but not the substance of a science."[25]

Wells's final statements:

My conclusion is that the case for Darwinian evolution is bankrupt. . . . The evidence for Darwinism is not only grossly inadequate, it's systematically distorted. I'm convinced that sometime in the not-too-distant future . . . people will look back in amazement and say, "How could anyone have believed this?" Darwinism is merely materialistic philosophy masquerading as science, and people are recognizing it for what it is. . . . I believe science is pointing strongly toward design. To me, as a scientist, the development of an embryo cries out, "Design!" The Cambrian explosion—the sudden appearance of complex life, with no evidence of ancestors—is more consistent with design than evolution. Homology, in my opinion, is more compatible with design. The origin of life certainly cries out for a designer. None of these things make as much sense from a Darwinian perspective as they do from a design perspective . . . When you analyze all of the most current affirmative evidence from cosmology, physics, astronomy, biology, and so forth—well, I think you'll discover that the positive case for an intelligent designer becomes absolutely compelling.[26]

Bradley, the origin-of-life expert, made similar statements when Strobel interviewed him.

- Bradley . . . said that the mind-boggling difficulties in bridging the yawning gap between nonlife and life mean that there may very well be no potential of ever finding a theory for how life could have arisen spontaneously. That's why he's convinced that the "absolutely overwhelming evidence" points toward an intelligence behind life's creation.[27]
- If there isn't a natural explanation and there doesn't seem to be the potential of finding one, then I believe it's appropriate to look at a supernatural explanation. . . . I think that's the most reasonable inference based on the evidence.[28]

Following these two interviews, Strobel stated, "My materialistic philosophy had been built on a foundation that history has subsequently dismantled piece by piece."[29]

He went on to say, "I was left with an origin-of-life experiment whose results have been rendered meaningless; a Tree of Life that had been uprooted by the Biological Big Bang of the Cambrian explosion; doctored embryo drawings that don't reflect reality; and a fossil record that stubbornly refuses to yield the transitional forms crucial to evolutionary theory. Doubts piled on doubts."[30] His final statement following these two interviews: "As for me, I finally came to the point where I realized that I just didn't have enough faith to maintain my belief in Darwinism. The evidence, in my estimation, was simply unable to support its grandest and most sweeping claims."[31]

Next stop

Strobel's next stop was an interview with Stephen Meyer, whose expertise lies in the area of the philosophy of science. Some of Meyer's words during that interview were:

- There's no question that science does teach us many important things about the natural world. But the real question is, "Do these things point to anything beyond themselves?" I think the answer is yes. Science teaches us many true things, and some of those true things point toward God.[32]
- Scientific evidence actually supports theistic belief. In fact, across a wide range of the sciences, evidence has come to light in the last fifty years

which, taken together, provides a robust case for theism. Only theism can provide an intellectually satisfying causal explanation for all of this evidence.[33]

- I believe that the testimony of science *supports* theism. While there will always be points of tension or unresolved conflict, the major developments in science in the past five decades have been running in a strongly theistic direction. . . . Science, *done right*, points toward God.[34]

- Biological machines need all of their various parts in order to function. But how could you ever build such a system by a Darwinian process of natural selection acting on random variations? Natural selection only preserves things that perform a function—in other words, which help the organism survive to the next generation. That's survival of the fittest. The problem with irreducibly complex systems is that they perform no function until all the parts are present and working together in close coordination with one another. So natural selection cannot help you build such systems; it can only preserve them once they've been built. And it's virtually impossible for evolution to take such a huge leap by mere chance to create the whole system at once."[35]

Strobel then went on to interview William Lane Craig, the cosmologist, who said:

- Predictions about the Big Bang have been consistently verified by scientific data. Moreover, they have been corroborated by the failure of every attempt to falsify them by alternative models. Unquestionably, the Big Bang model has impressive scientific credentials ... The Big Bang was not a chaotic, disorderly event. Instead, it appears to have been fine-tuned for the existence of intelligent life with a complexity and precision that literally defies human comprehension ... The universe we see today . . . depends upon a set of highly special initial conditions. This phenomenon is strong evidence that the Big Bang was not an accident, but that it was designed.[36]

- Given that whatever begins to exist has a cause and that the universe began to exist, there must be some sort of transcendent cause for the origin of the universe. . . . This is an inescapable conclusion—and it's a stunning confirmation of the millennia-old Judeo-Christian doctrine of creation out of nothing.[37]

- Because the cause of the universe transcends time and space, it cannot be a physical reality. Instead, it must be non-physical or immaterial. . . . A mind can be a cause, and so it makes sense that the universe is the product of an unembodied mind that brought it into existence.[38]

- Theories designed to avoid the beginning of the universe have either turned out to be untenable, like the Steady State theory, or else they imply the very beginning of the universe that their proponents have been desperately trying to avoid.[39]

- I think it's indisputable that there has never been a time in history when the hard evidence of science was more confirmatory of belief in God than today.[40]

Strobel's next interview was with Robin Collins, whose expertise is in physics and philosophy. Collins's statements during that interview include the following:

- When scientists talk about the fine-tuning of the universe . . . they're generally referring to the extraordinary balancing of the fundamental laws and parameters of physics and the initial conditions of the universe. Our minds can't comprehend the precision of some of them. The result is a universe that has just the right conditions to sustain life.[41]
- It's supremely improbable that the fine-tuning of the universe could have occurred at random, but it's not at all improbable if it were the work of an intelligent designer. So it's quite reasonable to choose the design theory over the chance theory."[42]
- We already know that intelligent minds produce finely tuned devices. Look at the space shuttle. Look at a television set. Look at an internal combustion engine. We see minds producing complex, precision machinery all the time. So postulating the existence of a supermind—or

God as the explanation for the fine-tuning of the universe makes all the sense in the world. It would simply be a natural extrapolation of what we already know that minds can do.[43]

- I see physics as uncovering the evidence of God's fingerprint at a deeper and more subtle level than the ancients could have dreamed of. He has used physics to enable me to see the evidence of his presence and creative ability. The heavens really do declare the glory of God, even more so for someone trained with physics and with eyes to see.[44]

Strobel's statement after his interview with Collins:

Whichever way I looked, the inference of design seemed inescapable. If ours is the only universe in existence, which is a logical conclusion based on the evidence, then its highly sophisticated fine-tuning cries out for a designer. On the other hand, if the esoteric theories of physicists turn out to be true and our universe is one of many others, then the need for a universe-generating mechanism also would demand a designer. Heads or tails, the Creator wins.[45]

Next leg

The next leg of Strobel's quest for answers was to interview Guillermo Gonzalez, astronomer, and Jay Wesley Richards, philosopher and theologian. That interview yielded the following comments:

- *Gonzalez:*

  We've found that our location in the universe, in our galaxy, in our solar system, as well as such things as the size and rotation of the earth, the mass of the moon and sun and so forth—a whole range of factors—conspire together in an amazing way to make Earth a habitable planet. . . . And even beyond that, we've found that the very same conditions that allow for intelligent life on Earth also make it strangely well-suited for viewing and analyzing the universe.[46]

- *Richards:*

  The same conditions that give us a habitable planet also make our location so wonderful for scientific measurement and discovery. So we say there's a correlation between habitability and measurability . . . We believe that the conditions for making scientific discoveries on Earth are so fine-tuned that you would need a great amount of faith to attribute them to mere chance.[47]

Following his interview with Gonzalez and Richards, Strobel stated, "If God so precisely and carefully and lovingly and amazingly constructed a mind-boggling habitat for his creatures, then it would be natural for him to want them to explore it, to measure it, to investigate it, to appreciate it, to be inspired by it—and ultimately, and most importantly, to find him through it.[48]

From here he went to interview Michael Behe, the biochemist. "After all, life is essentially a molecular phenomenon. If Darwinian evolution is going to work, it has to succeed at the microscopic level of amino acids, proteins, and DNA. On the other hand, if there really was a designer of the world, then his fingerprints were going to be all over the cell."[49]

Some of Behe's comments during the interview are as follows:

- The system of blood clotting involves a highly choreographed cascade of ten steps that use about twenty different molecular components. Without the whole system in place, it doesn't work. . . . The real trick with blood clotting isn't so much the clot itself . . . It's the regulation of the system. . . . To create a perfectly balanced blood-clotting system, clusters of protein components have to be inserted all at once. That rules out a gradualistic Darwinian approach and fits the hypothesis of an intelligent designer.[50]

- Right now, there's only one principle that we know can come up with complex interactive systems, and that's intelligence. Natural selection has been proposed, but there's little or no evidence backing that claim. Some people had high hopes for self-organizational properties or complexity theories, but there's no evidence that these can explain something as complicated as the cell. The only force known to be able to make irreducibly complex machines is intelligent design.[51]

At this point in his process, or on his quest, Strobel paused to take stock of where he was and stated: "Connecting the dots from my interviews with William Lane Craig, Robin Collins, Guillermo Gonzalez, Jay Richards, and Michael Behe, I was coming up with a picture that was squarely at odds with the icons that had once led me into atheism.[52]

He then interviewed Stephen Meyer for a second time, as Meyer had studied DNA extensively. DNA, stated Meyer, is "the information storehouse for a finely choreographed manufacturing process in which the right amino acids are linked together with the right bonds in the right sequence to produce the right kind of proteins that fold in the right way to build biological systems."[53]

Meyer stated, "The origin of information in DNA—which is necessary for life to begin—is best explained by an intelligent cause rather than any of the types of naturalistic causes that scientists typically use to explain biological phenomena."[54] He went on to say that the origin of that information is "*the* critical and foundational question. If you can't explain where the information comes from, you haven't explained life, because it's the information that makes the molecules into something that actually functions. . . . I believe the presence of information in the cell is best explained by the activity of an intelligent agent."[55]

Meyer's additional comments included:

- Darwinists admit that natural selection requires a self-replicating organism to work. . . . Organisms reproduce, their offspring have variations, the ones that are better adapted to their environment survive better, and so those adaptations are preserved and passed on to the next generation. However, to have reproduction, there has to be cell division. And that presupposes the existence of information-rich DNA and proteins. . . . In other words, you've got to have a self-replicating organism for Darwinian evolution to take place, but you can't have a self-replicating organism until you have the information necessary in DNA. [56]

- The coding regions of DNA have *exactly* the same relevant properties as a computer code or language . . . Whenever you find a sequential arrangement that's complex and corresponds to an independent pattern or functional requirement, this kind of information is *always* the product of intelligence. Books, computer codes, and DNA all have these two properties. We know books and computer codes are designed by intelligence, and the presence of this type of information in DNA also implies an intelligent source.[57]

- Naturalism cannot answer the fundamental problem of how to get from matter and energy to biological function without the infusion of information from an intelligence.[58]

Final interview

Strobel ended his quest by interviewing J. P. Moreland, an expert in the area of human consciousness. Strobel's rational for this interview is as follows:

- According to Darwinists, the physical world is all that there is. At some point, the human brain evolved, with its raw processing power increasing over the eons. When the brain reached a certain level of structure and complexity, people became "conscious"—that is, they suddenly developed subjectivity, feelings, hopes, a point of view, self-awareness, introspection, that "hidden voice of our private selves."[59]

Some of Moreland's additional statements include:

- *You can't get something from nothing. . . .* It's as simple as that. If there were no God, then the history of the entire universe, up until the appearance of living creatures, would be a history of dead matter with no consciousness. You would not have any thoughts, beliefs, feelings, sensations, free actions, choices, or purposes. There would be simply one physical event after another physical event, behaving according to the laws of physics and chemistry. . . . How, then, do you get something totally different— conscious, living, thinking, feeling, believing creatures—from materials that don't have that? That's getting something from nothing! And that's the main problem.[60]
- To explain something scientifically, you've got to show *why* the phenomenon *had* to happen given the causes. And scientists cannot explain the "why"

behind consciousness, because there's no necessary connection between the brain and consciousness. It didn't have to happen this way. [61]

At the end of his quest Strobel reached the following conclusions and made the following decisions:

- The facts of science systematically eroded the foundation of Darwinism until it could no longer support the weight of my atheistic conclusions. Suddenly, the intellectual basis for my skepticism was collapsing. That was disconcerting enough. But then . . . my wide-ranging research was building an unexpected affirmative case for the existence of a Creator. Yes, I was stunned; yes, I felt like the wind was being knocked out of me; yes, it was unnerving to wrestle with the implications. But I had vowed to follow the facts regardless of the cost—even at the cost of my own smug self-sufficiency.[62]
- As I reviewed the avalanche of information from my investigation, I found the evidence for an intelligent designer to be credible, cogent, and compelling. Actually, in my opinion the combination of the findings from cosmology and physics by themselves were sufficient to support the design hypothesis. All of the other data simply built an even more powerful cumulative case that ended up overwhelming my objections . . . The portrait of the Creator that emerges

from the scientific data is uncannily consistent with the description of the God whose identity is spelled out in the pages of the Bible.[63]

- To me, the range, the variety, the depth, and the breathtaking persuasive power of the evidence from both science and history affirmed the credibility of Christianity to the degree that my doubts were simply washed away.[64]

- Putting my trust in the God of the Bible was nothing less than the most rational and natural decision I could make. I was merely permitting the torrent of facts to carry me along to their most logical conclusion. . . . I see faith as being a reasonable step in the same direction that the evidence is pointing. In other words, faith goes beyond merely acknowledging that the facts of science and history point toward God. It's responding to those facts by investing trust in God—a step that's fully warranted due to the supporting evidence.[65]

- The facts of science and history, then, can only take us so far. At some point, the truth demands a response. When we decide not merely to ponder the abstract concept of a designer but to embrace him as our own—to make him our "true God"—then we can meet him personally, relate to him daily, and spend eternity with him as he promises.[66]

The following words of Stephen Meyer seem to me to tie it all together: "Science and faith are not at war. When scientific evidence and biblical teaching are correctly interpreted, they can and do support each other."[67]

Pressing the pause button

I hope that by now you are, at the very least, considering the possibility that God is real and that he created the universe and everything in it. I have laid out quite a bit of evidence that points to the existence of a superior being or higher power, aka, God. I am now going to ask you to shift gears, turn around, and, rather than looking outside yourself for proof that God exists, look inside yourself to see what is stopping you from believing in God.

Lee Strobel explained what stopped him from believing in God in his early years. "In a world without God, I reveled in my newly achieved freedom from God's moral strictures. For me, living without God meant living one hundred percent for myself. Freed from someday being held accountable for my actions, I felt unleashed to pursue personal happiness and pleasure at all costs."[68]

I don't pretend to know all the reasons people choose not to believe in God. I am going to throw out a few possibilities, though. Maybe one of them will fit you.

- You don't want to give up control of your life.
- Taking a leap of faith seems way too scary. You find it difficult to believe anything you can't see.
- Adopting beliefs different from what you were taught growing up seems like a betrayal of your parents and family of origin.

CHAPTER THREE

GOD'S FAMILY

It is important to realize that God did not create the universe and everything in it, including human beings, and then go back to heaven and stay there, leaving us on our own. No! From the beginning of time, God invited the human beings he created to be in relationship with him. He always has and always will be available to be in relationship with anyone who chooses to enter into a relationship with him. As a matter of fact, he rejoices when anyone makes this choice, becoming part of his family.

The story of God's relationship with the human race is told in the Bible. The Bible is a factual account of actual occurrences and real people's lives. It is not a myth, a legend, or a fictitious story. (The reliability, or historicity, of the Bible is addressed in chapter six.)

God's intention and desire for relationship seems evident in his interactions with the first man and woman he created. "When the cool evening breezes were blowing, the man and his wife heard the Lord God walking about in the garden. So they hid from the Lord God among the trees. Then the Lord God called to the man, 'Where are you?'" (Genesis 3:8–9). Presumably, God wanted to walk with them in the garden. God changed his mind, however, because they had disobeyed him by eating fruit from the one tree he had told them not to touch. "So the LORD God banished them from the Garden of Eden, and he sent Adam out to cultivate the ground from which he had been made" (Genesis 3:23).

After Adam and Eve left the garden, the human race grew and multiplied and became very evil.

> The LORD observed the extent of human wickedness on the earth, and he saw that everything they thought or imagined was consistently and totally evil. So the LORD was sorry he had ever made them and put them on the earth. It broke his heart. And the LORD said, "I will wipe this human race I have created from the face of the earth. Yes, and I will destroy every living thing—all the people, the large animals, the small animals that scurry along the ground, and even the birds of the sky. I am sorry I ever made them." But Noah found favor with the LORD. (Genesis 6:5–8)

God told Noah that he planned to destroy the evil human race with a great flood. He then instructed Noah to build a boat, as he intended to save Noah and his family from the flood. When the boat was completed according to the exact specifications God had given to Noah, God told Noah to board the boat with his family and two of every species of bird, mammal, and reptile.

God then made it rain for forty days and forty nights. Floodwaters covered the earth, killing every living thing. God then brought wind, and the wind began to reverse the flood. When the flood waters receded, "Noah disembarked with his sons and wife and his sons' wives. Then all the animals, crawling creatures, birds—every creature on the face of the Earth—left the ship family by family" (Genesis 8:18–19 MSG).

The human race once again grew and multiplied. God then created a people who were set apart to belong to him, to be his family. God chose Abraham to be the father of his family. God promised Abraham that he would have many descendants and that these descendants would form many nations. Further, God promised Abraham that he would provide a home for his descendants. "This is the everlasting covenant: I will always be your God and the God of your descendants after you. And I will give the entire land of Canaan, where you now live as a foreigner, to you and your descendants. It will be their possession forever, and I will be their God" (Genesis 17:7–8).

God also gave Abraham a vision of what would happen to his descendants long after his death. "'Know this: your descendants will live as outsiders in a land not theirs; they'll be enslaved and beaten down for 400 years. Then I'll punish their slave masters; your offspring will march out of there loaded with plunder'" (Genesis 15:13–14 MSG).

The land "not theirs" that Abraham's descendants would end up in was Egypt. When God was ready to bring his family, the Israelites, out of slavery in Egypt, he chose Moses to lead them.

God protected his family

When the Israelites left Egypt, "GOD kept watch all night, watching over the Israelites as he brought them out of Egypt" (Exodus 12:41 MSG). God never left them. He continued to keep watch over them and lead them on their journey. "GOD went ahead of them in a Pillar of Cloud during the day to guide them on the way, and at night in a Pillar of Fire to give them light; thus they could travel both day and night. The Pillar of Cloud by day and the Pillar of Fire by night never left the people" (Exodus 13:21–22 MSG).

Throughout the long, difficult years of the journey, God never abandoned Moses. He listened to Moses and guided him as to what to do and when to do it.

When they reached the promised land, God told Moses he was about to die, and Moses, per God's instruction, commissioned Joshua to be his successor.

When the Israelites entered the promised land, they were faced with many walled cities full of enemies. The Israelites, led by Joshua, captured each of the enemy cities one by one. Eventually, the Israelites overcame all their enemies and possessed the land, settling into their lives in the land God had promised them long before.

After Joshua died, the people were led by a series of prophets and judges, many of whom were godly leaders. The people eventually grew tired of this style of leadership and asked to have a king so they could be like the nations around them. Saul was the first king, David the second, and Solomon the third.

Later in his life Solomon drifted away from God and began to worship other gods. He began to drift when he chose to love and marry non-Israelite women, something God had forbidden. God specifically instructed the people of Israel not to marry outside their faith for fear that foreigners would turn the hearts of the Israelites to other gods, and that is exactly what happened with Solomon. Like Adam and Eve, Solomon chose to do what he wanted, not what God had commanded. Because of the choices Solomon made, when he died God split the nation of Israel into two kingdoms—the northern kingdom (Israel) and the southern kingdom (Judah).

The people of both kingdoms continued to ignore God's commands, refusing to live their lives according to his rules. God tried for a long time to get his people back on track by sending many leaders and prophets to help them and to warn them. Though some of these godly leaders were able to lead the Israelites back to God, the people never stayed there for very long. They continually drifted back into doing whatever they wanted, ignoring God's rules and expectations. God finally had enough and decided that his people, his children, needed serious discipline.

God disciplined his children

God chose destruction and exile as his methods of disciplining his children. He exiled the northern kingdom (Israel) to Assyria, and sometime later he exiled the southern kingdom (Judah) to Babylon. Though he sent his people into exile, he did not abandon them. He stayed connected to them and communicated with them through the prophets Ezekiel, Isaiah, and Jeremiah. These prophets conveyed to the exiles God's messages of encouragement and hope, as well as promises of restoration.

When God was ready to bring his people home once the disciplining process was over, he chose the pagan king of Persia, King Cyrus, as his instrument for doing so. Though Cyrus paved the way for the Jewish people to return to their homeland, many chose not to do that. They therefore remained scattered throughout the known world.

The Jews who did return to their homeland, particularly the leaders, were determined to start over by not repeating the mistakes and sins of their past. The experience of having lived through war, destruction, captivity, and exile led many of them to embrace radical obedience as a major component of their faith. God's people had lost sight of God's original purpose in giving them rules to live by.

Reason for the rules

When God gave the Israelites rules to live by (the Ten Commandments) after he brought them out of slavery in Egypt, he was taking care of them, protecting them. He never meant for the rules to replace the relationship he had with them. As a matter of fact, God gave the Israelites rules to highlight and enhance his relationship with them. He wanted the Israelites to be set apart from the nations surrounding them. He wanted them to live by a higher standard than the people around them so they would be identified by themselves and other nations as his people, his family. God did not want the Israelites to follow his rules so that they could *become* his children. They *already were* his children. He wanted them to follow his rules so that the world would *know* they were his children.

They lost sight of the purpose for the rules, however, when they were sent into exile. Their view of God as a loving parent who would take care of them changed to a view of God as an angry parent who would punish them if they disobeyed him. This led them to shift their focus from their relationship with God to the rules he had given them. They put their trust in the rules and in their own ability to follow them, rather than putting their trust in God.

When the Israelites lost sight of the reason for the rules God had given them, and then started acting accordingly, *religion* was born. They moved from being dependent on God to being dependent on themselves, on their own rule keeping. This is the very essence of religion.

This grieved God, so much so that he sent his Son, Jesus Christ, to earth to restore what had been lost: a personal relationship between God and human beings. Jesus became the bridge between human beings and God, doing for us what we were unable to do for ourselves.

Important note: When I speak of religion, I am not referring to any particular denomination or group. I am referring to "any system of rules, regulations, rituals, and routines that people use to achieve their spiritual end-goal."[69]

CHAPTER FOUR

JESUS: THE BRIDGE

Throughout the three years of his earthly ministry, Jesus consistently loved people and taught that love was more important than obedience to the Jewish law (the Ten Commandments God had given Moses, plus more than 2,000 additional laws the Jewish leaders had developed to help people keep the Ten Commandments). He also taught that following the rules will not get one to heaven. He continually told people that the way to God and to eternal life was not religion (obeying the law); it was relationship (believing that he was who he said he was, the Son of God, and following him). He consistently pointed to himself as the way to heaven.

When speaking with his disciple Nathanael, Jesus said, "I tell you the truth, you will all see heaven open and the angels of God going up and down on the Son of Man, the one who is the stairway between heaven and earth" (John 1:51).

When talking to Martha, Jesus said, "I am the resurrection and the life. Anyone who believes in me will live, even after dying. Everyone who lives in me and believes in me will never ever die" (John 11:25–26).

Five days before his death, Jesus said the following words to a crowd in Jerusalem: "If you trust me, you are trusting not only me, but also God who sent me. For when you see me, you are seeing the one who sent me. I have come as a light to shine in this dark world, so that all who put their trust in me will no longer remain in the dark" (John 12:44-46).

At the last meal Jesus shared with the apostles before his death, he again made the point that trusting in him, not in a set of rules or laws, is the way to God. He said, "Don't let your hearts be troubled. Trust in God, and trust also in me. . . . I am the way, the truth, and the life. No one can come to the Father except through me" (John 14:1, 6).

The Jewish leaders, needless to say, were outraged at Jesus for his constant challenging of their core beliefs, and they eventually arranged the circumstances that led to his crucifixion. Jesus had foretold his crucifixion in a dialogue with Nicodemus, a Jewish religious leader, when he stated, "The Son of Man must be lifted up, so that everyone who believes in him will have eternal life" (John 3:14–15).

Why did Jesus have to die on a cross?

In order to understand why Jesus had to die on a cross, we need to go back to when the Israelites were set free from slavery in Egypt.

Two months after they left Egypt, the Israelites arrived at Mount Sinai and set up camp at the base of the mountain. While they were there, God gave Moses the Ten Commandments. He also instructed Moses to have the people build a portable tabernacle, or tent, in which they could worship him while they were on their journey. One of the furnishings for the tabernacle was an altar upon which animals would be sacrificed as an offering to atone for sin.

During one of the conversations between God and Moses, God explained to Moses why the killing of animals was necessary to atone for sin: "For the life of the body is in its blood. I have given you the blood on the altar to purify you, making you right with the LORD. It is the blood, given in exchange for a life, that makes purification possible" (Leviticus 17:11).

The sacrificing of animals needed to be continually repeated because these blood sacrifices, or burnt offerings, atoned for sin only partially and for a short time. When Christ shed his blood on the cross, however, it was a once for all time sacrifice, making future sacrifices unnecessary. He was the Lamb of God, the perfect sacrifice God provided that would make all future animal sacrifices unnecessary. The blood of bulls and goats and lambs was no longer needed to cleanse people from their sins. Jesus's blood covers all who accept his free gift of salvation, forgiving all their sins—past, present and future—for all time.

Jesus's final act of love for humanity, while in his earthly body, was allowing himself to be crucified. If you want a picture of pure, perfect love, visualize Jesus, bloody and beaten beyond recognition, hanging on a wooden cross. He did not have to stay hanging there. He *chose* to stay hanging there. It was not nails that held him to that cross. It was love, love for each and every one of us, past, present, and future.

It is important to note that Jesus went to the cross out of obedience to his Father and love for us. It was a choice he made *in spite of* how he was feeling. Prior to his arrest, Jesus spoke to the apostles about the choice he was making. He said, "No one can take my life from me. I sacrifice it voluntarily. For I have the authority to lay it down when I want to and also to take it up again. For this is what my Father has commanded" (John 10:18). He also stated, "There is no greater love than to lay down one's life for one's friends" (John 15:13).

Jesus's act of love

When he and his apostles finished the last meal they would eat together, Jesus, knowing he was about to be arrested, went to the Garden of Gethsemane to pray.

> He walked away, about a stone's throw, and knelt down and prayed, "Father, if you are willing, please take this cup of suffering away from me. Yet I want your will to be done, not mine." Then an angel from heaven appeared and strengthened him. He prayed more fervently, and he was in such agony of spirit that his sweat fell to the ground like great drops of blood. (Luke 22:41–44)

As Jesus finished praying, he was arrested by Jewish authorities and taken to the home of the high priest.

> Inside, the leading priests and the entire high council were trying to find evidence against Jesus, so they could put him to death. . . . Finally, some

men stood up and gave this false testimony: "We heard him say, 'I will destroy this Temple made with human hands, and in three days I will build another, made without human hands.'". . .

Then the high priest stood up before the others and asked Jesus, "Well, aren't you going to answer these charges? What do you have to say for yourself?" But Jesus was silent and made no reply. Then the high priest asked him, "Are you the Messiah? The Son of the Blessed One?"

Jesus said, "I AM. And you will see the Son of Man seated in the place of power at God's right hand and coming on the clouds of heaven." (Mark 14:55, 57–58, 60–62)

Following this, the Jewish leaders took Jesus to the Roman governor, Pontius Pilate, because they did not have the authority to sentence him to death. Pilate questioned Jesus regarding the charges the Jewish leaders were bringing against him but was unable to find Jesus guilty of any crime. The crowd meanwhile continued to insist, in ever increasing volume and intensity, that Jesus be crucified. "So to pacify the crowd, Pilate . . . ordered Jesus flogged with a lead-tipped whip, then turned him over to the Roman soldiers to be crucified" (Mark 15:15).

To give you an idea of what Roman floggings in the first century were like:

Roman floggings were known to be terribly brutal. They usually consisted of thirty-nine lashes but frequently were a lot more than that, depending on the mood of the soldier applying the blows. The soldier would use a whip of braided leather thongs with metal balls woven into them. When the whip would strike the flesh, these balls would cause deep bruises or contusions, which would break open with further blows. And the whip had pieces of sharp bone as well, which would cut the flesh severely. The back would be so shredded that part of the spine was sometimes exposed by the deep, deep cuts. The whipping would have gone all the way from the shoulders down to the back, the buttocks, and the back of the legs.[70]

Jesus was then ordered to carry the cross upon which he would die to the site of the crucifixion. Due to the extreme pain he was in and the extensive blood loss from the flogging, he was unable to do this and collapsed. "As they led Jesus away, a man named Simon, who was from Cyrene, happened to be coming in from the countryside. The soldiers seized him and put the cross on him and made him carry it behind Jesus" (Luke 23:26).

Alexander Metherell, a medical doctor in southern California who has studied the historical, archaeological, and medical evidence regarding Jesus's death, explains what Jesus likely experienced once he reached the site of the crucifixion:

He would have been laid down, and his hands would have been nailed in the outstretched position to the horizontal beam . . . At this stage it was separate from the vertical beam, which was permanently set in the ground. . . . The Romans used spikes that were five to seven inches long and tapered to a sharp point. They were driven through the wrists. . . . This was a solid position that would lock the hand; if the nails had been driven through the palms, his weight would have caused the skin to tear and he would fallen off the cross . . . It's important to understand that the nail would go through the place where the median nerve runs. This is the largest nerve going out to the hand, and it would be crushed by the nail that was being pounded in. . . . The pain was absolutely unbearable. . . . In fact, it was literally beyond words to describe; they had to invent a new word: *excruciating.* Literally, *excruciating* means "out of the cross." . . . At this point Jesus was hoisted as the crossbar was attached to the vertical stake, and then nails were driven through Jesus' feet. Again, the nerves in his feet would have been crushed, and there would have been a similar type of pain.[71]

Metherell went on to explain the impact hanging on the cross would have had on Jesus's body:

First of all, his arms would have immediately been stretched, probably about six inches in length, and both shoulders would have become dislocated. . . . Once a person is hanging in a vertical position crucifixion is essentially an agonizingly slow death by asphyxiation . . . The stresses on the muscles and diaphragm put the chest into the inhaled position;

basically, in order to exhale, the individual must push up on his feet so the tension on the muscles would be eased for a moment. In doing so, the nail would tear through the foot, eventually locking up against the tarsal bones. After managing to exhale, the person would then be able to relax down and take another breath in. Again he'd have to push himself up to exhale, scraping his bloodied back against the coarse wood of the cross. This would go on and on until complete exhaustion would take over, and the person wouldn't be able to push up and breathe anymore. As the person slows down his breathing, he goes into what is called respiratory acidosis—the carbon dioxide in the blood is dissolved as carbonic acid, causing the acidity of the blood to increase. This eventually leads to an irregular heartbeat. In fact, with his heart beating erratically, Jesus would have known that he was at the moment of death, which is when he was able to say, "Lord, into your hands I commit my spirit." And then he died of cardiac arrest.[72]

Personal note

Reading Dr. Metherell's account of Jesus's flogging and crucifixion was very difficult emotionally for me. Writing about it was even more difficult. It gave me a deeper and more thorough understanding of what Jesus did for us. I am absolutely astounded at the choices he made. First of all, in spite of the overwhelming anxiety and severe psychological stress he was experiencing in the Garden of Gethsemane, he agreed to abide by his Father's will and fulfill the purpose for which he had become human and come to earth. Then he did not defend himself to either the Jewish high council or the Roman governor. *Then* he remained nailed to the cross.

Again, Jesus did not have to stay hanging on that cross. He *chose* to stay hanging there. It was not Roman nails that held him to that cross; it was love, love for each and every one of us, past, present, and future. His action of staying nailed to that cross until he died was a gift of love for all people throughout time, including the people who crucified him and those who mocked and abused him as he hung on the cross.

> The people passing by shouted abuse, shaking their heads in mockery. "Look at you now!" they yelled at him. "You said you were going to destroy the Temple and rebuild it in three days. Well then, if you are the Son of God, save yourself and come down from the cross!"
>
> The leading priests, the teachers of religious law, and the elders also mocked Jesus. "He saved others," they scoffed, "but he can't save himself! So he is the King of Israel, is he? Let him come down from the cross right now, and we will believe in him! He trusted God, so let God rescue him now if he wants him! For he said, 'I am the Son of God.'" Even the revolutionaries who were crucified with him ridiculed him in the same way. (Matthew 27:39–44)

What the leading priests, teachers of religious law, and elders did not understand was that Jesus stayed on that cross *for them.* If Jesus had come down from that cross, which he was more than capable of doing, he would have saved himself. He would not, however, have saved them, and he would not have saved us. No one else has ever or will ever love you this much. And this is not the end of the story . . .

The rest of the story

Afterward Joseph of Arimathea, who had been a secret disciple of Jesus (because he feared the Jewish leaders), asked Pilate for permission to take down Jesus' body. When Pilate gave permission, Joseph came and took the body away. With him came Nicodemus, the man who had come to Jesus at night. He brought about seventy-five pounds of perfumed ointment made from myrrh and aloes. Following Jewish burial custom, they wrapped Jesus' body with the spices in long sheets of linen cloth. The place of crucifixion was near a garden, where there was a new tomb, never used before. And so, because it was the day of preparation for the Jewish Passover and since the tomb was close at hand, they laid Jesus there. (John 19:38–42)

Early on Sunday morning, while it was still dark, Mary Magdalene came to the tomb and found that the stone had been rolled away from the entrance. She ran and found Simon Peter and the other disciple, the one whom Jesus loved. She said,

"They have taken the Lord's body out of the tomb, and we don't know where they have put him!"

Peter and the other disciple started out for the tomb. They were both running, but the other disciple outran Peter and reached the tomb first. He stooped and looked in and saw the linen wrappings lying there, but he didn't go in. Then Simon Peter arrived and went inside. He also noticed the linen wrappings lying there, while the cloth that had covered Jesus' head was folded up and lying apart from the other wrappings. Then the disciple who had reached the tomb first also went in, and he saw and believed—for until then they still hadn't understood the Scriptures that said Jesus must rise from the dead. (John 20:1–9)

There were numerous instances in which Jesus had been telling the disciples about his impending crucifixion and subsequent resurrection from the dead. Some of these instances were:

- After they gathered again in Galilee, Jesus told them, "The Son of Man is going to be betrayed into the hands of his enemies. He will be killed, but on the third day he will be raised from the dead." And the disciples were filled with grief. (Matthew 17:22–23)
- As Jesus was going up to Jerusalem, he took the twelve disciples aside privately and told them

what was going to happen to him. "Listen," he said, "we're going up to Jerusalem, where the Son of Man will be betrayed to the leading priests and the teachers of religious law. They will sentence him to die. Then they will hand him over to the Romans to be mocked, flogged with a whip, and crucified. But on the third day he will be raised from the dead." (Matthew 20:17–19)

- "But after I have been raised from the dead, I will go ahead of you to Galilee and meet you there." (Matthew 26:32)

Jesus kept the promise he made to his disciples. "During the forty days after he suffered and died, he appeared to the apostles from time to time, and he proved to them in many ways that he was actually alive. And he talked to them about the Kingdom of God" (Acts 1:3).

Significance of the resurrection

The empty tomb, as an enduring symbol of the resurrection, is the ultimate representation of Jesus' claim to being God. The Apostle Paul said in 1 Corinthians 15:17 that the resurrection is the very linchpin of the Christian faith: "If Christ has not been raised, your faith is futile; you are still in your sins." Theologian Gerald O'Collins put it this way: "In a profound sense, Christianity without the resurrection is not simply Christianity without its final chapter. It is not Christianity at all." The resurrection

is the supreme vindication of Jesus' divine
identity and his inspired teaching. It's the
proof of his triumph over sin and death. It's
the foreshadowing of the resurrection of his
followers. It's the basis of Christian hope. It's
the miracle of all miracles.[73]

William Lane Craig writes:

It is quite clear that without the belief in the
resurrection the Christian faith could not have
come into being. The disciples would have
remained crushed and defeated men. Even
had they continued to remember Jesus as their
believed teacher, His crucifixion would have
forever silenced any hopes of His being the
Messiah. The cross could have remained the
sad and shameful end to His career. The origin
of Christianity therefore hinges on the belief
of the early disciples that God had raised Jesus
from the dead.[74]

In addition, the resurrection is a clear indication of
the afterlife. Another indication of the afterlife is Jesus's
words to one of the criminals crucified next to him.

Two others, both criminals, were led out to be
executed with him. When they came to a place
called The Skull, they nailed him to the cross.
And the criminals were also crucified—one on
his right and one on his left. . . .

One of the criminals hanging beside him scoffed, "So you're the Messiah, are you? Prove it by saving yourself—and us, too, while you're at it!"

But the other criminal protested, "Don't you fear God even when you have been sentenced to die? We deserve to die for our crimes, but this man hasn't done anything wrong." Then he said, "Jesus, remember me when you come into your Kingdom."

And Jesus replied, "I assure you, today you will be with me in paradise." (Luke 23:32–33, 39–43)

Special note

I want to say a word to those of you who were raised in the Jewish faith. If you are still waiting for the Messiah, I urge you to consider the possibility that Jesus *is* the Messiah. I realize this contradicts what you were taught growing up; however, there are more than forty prophecies about the coming Messiah in the Hebrew Bible, known to Christians as the Old Testament, all of which Jesus fulfilled. I will share a smattering of them with you, along with the New Testament verses testifying to their fulfillment. I also encourage you to do your own research. Don't take my word or anyone else's word, for that matter, that Jesus is or is not the Messiah.

The royal line of David is like a tree that has been cut down; but just as new branches sprout from a stump, so a new king will arise from among David's descendants. (Isaiah 11:1 TEV)

He will be very great and will be called the Son of the Most High. The Lord God will give him the throne of his ancestor David. And he will reign over Israel forever; his Kingdom will never end! (Luke 1:32–33)

But you, O Bethlehem Ephrathah, are only a small village among all the people of Judah. Yet a ruler of Israel, whose origins are in the distant past, will come from you on my behalf. (Micah 5:2)

And because Joseph was a descendant of King David, he had to go to Bethlehem in Judea, David's ancient home. He traveled there from the village of Nazareth in Galilee. He took with him Mary, to whom he was engaged, who was now expecting a child. And while they were there, the time came for her baby to be born. She gave birth to her firstborn son. She wrapped him snugly in strips of cloth and laid him in a manger, because there was no lodging available for them. (Luke 2:4–7)

The Lord himself will give you the sign. Look! The virgin will conceive a child! She will give birth to a son and will call him Immanuel (which means "God is with us"). (Isaiah 7:14)

This is how Jesus the Messiah was born. His mother, Mary, was engaged to be married to Joseph. But before the marriage took place, while she was still a virgin, she became pregnant through the power of the Holy Spirit. (Matthew 1:18)

She gave birth to her firstborn son. She wrapped him snugly in strips of cloth and laid him in a manger, because there was no lodging available for them. That night there were shepherds staying in the fields nearby, guarding their flocks of sheep. Suddenly, an angel of the Lord appeared among them, and the radiance of the Lord's glory surrounded them. They were terrified, but the angel reassured them. "Don't be afraid!" he said. "I bring you good news that will bring great joy to all people. The Savior—yes, the Messiah, the Lord—has been born today in Bethlehem, the city of David! And you will recognize him by this sign: You will find a baby wrapped snugly in strips of cloth, lying in a manger." (Luke: 2:7–12)

"Look! I am sending my messenger, and he will prepare the way before me. Then the Lord you are seeking will suddenly come to his Temple. The messenger of the covenant, whom you look for so eagerly, is surely coming," says the Lord of Heaven's Armies. (Malachi 3:1)

John is the man to whom the Scriptures refer when they say "Look, I am sending my messenger ahead of you, and he will prepare your way before you." (Matthew 11:10).

Listen! It's the voice of someone shouting, "Clear the way through the wilderness for the Lord! Make a straight highway through the wasteland for our God! Fill in the valleys, and level the mountains and hills. Straighten the curves, and smooth out the rough places. Then the glory of the Lord will be revealed, and all people will see it together. The Lord has spoken!" (Isaiah 40:3–5)

Then John went from place to place on both sides of the Jordan River, preaching that people should be baptized to show that they had repented of their sins and turned to God to be forgiven. Isaiah had spoken of John when he said, "He is a voice shouting in the wilderness, 'Prepare the way for the LORD's coming! Clear the road for him! The valleys will be filled, and the mountains and hills made level. The curves will be straightened, and the rough places made smooth. And then all people will see the salvation sent from God.'" (Luke 3:3–6)

O my people, listen to my instructions. Open your ears to what I am saying, for I will speak to you in a parable. I will teach you hidden lessons from our past. (Psalm 78:1–2)

He told many stories in the form of parables. (Matthew 13:3)

Say to those with fearful hearts, "Be strong and do not fear, for your God is coming to destroy your enemies. He is coming to save you." And when he comes, he will open the eyes of the blind and unplug the ears of the deaf. The lame will leap like a deer, and those who cannot speak will sing for joy! (Isaiah 35:4–6)

"What do you want me to do for you?" Jesus asked. "My Rabbi," the blind man said, "I want to see!" And Jesus said to him, "Go, for your faith has healed you." Instantly the man could see, and he followed Jesus down the road. (Mark 10:51–52)

A deaf man with a speech impediment was brought to him, and the people begged Jesus to lay his hands on the man to heal him. Jesus led him away from the crowd so they could be alone. He put his fingers into the man's ears. Then, spitting on his own fingers, he touched the man's tongue. Looking up to heaven, he sighed and said, "*Ephphatha*," which means "Be opened!" Instantly the man could hear perfectly, and his tongue was freed so he could speak plainly! (Mark 7:32–35)

Then Jesus turned to the paralyzed man and said, "Stand up, pick up your mat, and go home!" And the man jumped up, grabbed his mat, and walked out through the stunned onlookers. (Mark 2:10–12)

When they left, a demon-possessed man who couldn't speak was brought to Jesus. So Jesus cast out the demon, and then the man began to speak. (Matthew 9:32–33)

Rejoice, O People of Zion! Shout in triumph, O people of Jerusalem! Look, your king is coming to you. He is righteous and victorious, yet he is humble, riding on a donkey— riding on a donkey's colt. (Zechariah 9:9)

As Jesus and the disciples approached Jerusalem, they came to the town of Bethpage on the Mount of Olives. Jesus sent two of them on ahead. "Go into the village over there," he said. "As soon as you enter it, you will see a donkey tied there, with its colt beside it. Untie them and bring them to me.". . . The two disciples did as Jesus commanded. They brought the donkey and the colt to him and threw their garments over the colt, and he sat on it. Most of the crowd spread their garments on the road ahead of him, and others cut branches from the trees and spread them on the road. Jesus was in the center of the procession, and the people all around him were shouting, "Praise God for the Son of David! Blessings on the one who comes in the name of the LORD! Praise God in highest heaven!" (Matthew 21:1–2, 6–9)

And I said to them, "If you like, give me my wages, whatever I am worth; but only if you want to." So they counted out for my wages thirty pieces of silver. (Zechariah 11:12)

Then Judas Iscariot, one of the twelve disciples, went to the leading priests and asked, "How much will you pay me to betray Jesus to you?" And they gave him thirty pieces of silver. (Matthew 26:14–15)

He was oppressed and treated harshly, yet he never said a word. He was led like a lamb to the slaughter. And as a sheep is silent before the shearers, he did not open his mouth. (Isaiah 53:7)

Pilate asked him, "Aren't you going to answer them? What about all these charges they are bringing against you?" But Jesus said nothing, much to Pilate's surprise. (Mark 15:4–5)

My enemies surround me like a pack of dogs; an evil gang closes in on me. They have pierced my hands and feet. I can count all my bones. My enemies stare at me and gloat. They divide my garments among themselves and throw dice for my clothing. (Psalm 22:16–18)

After they had nailed him to the cross, the soldiers gambled for his clothes by throwing dice. (Matthew 27:35)

Pressing the pause button again

Before I move on to discussing the afterlife, I am pushing the pause button again. Believing that God exists, though it may be a huge step for some, is not quite enough to spend eternity with him. If you choose to believe that God exists and you want to spend eternity with him, you have to become part of his family. You do this by believing that Jesus truly is the Son of God and by accepting his gift of love, thereby having a personal relationship with him. There is no other way. Let me ask you this: Would you invite someone into your home to stay there forever if you did not have a relationship with him or her? I wouldn't.

If you truly believe that Jesus suffered all of the above for you, taking your place, paying the penalty for all your sins and wrongdoings so you wouldn't have to, what is stopping you from giving your life to him and making him the Lord of your life?

Again, though I don't pretend to know all the reasons people choose not to accept Jesus's gift of love and give their life to him, I am going to again throw out a few possibilities. Maybe one of them will resonate with you.

- You have never experienced unconditional love, so it is hard for you to believe someone could love you this much.
- You are afraid to give away control of your life.
- You have known Christians who are mean, vindictive, selfish, immoral, hypocritical, etc. In response to this I remind you that: (a) people, including Christians, are broken; (b) not everyone

who claims to be a Christian is *actually* a Christian; and (c) we do not follow people; we follow Christ.

- You refuse to believe that a personal relationship with Jesus is the *only* way to God and heaven. If this one resonates with you, the following words of Sean McDowell are for you:

One of the most common questions we both receive is, "How can you say Jesus is the only way to God?". . . Recently I was in a conversation with a friend, and he asked how I could say that Jesus is the only way. I simply said, "I'm not saying it. Jesus said it. [I am the way, the truth, and the life. No one can come to the Father except through me (John 14:6).] Take it up with him." . . . My point was Jesus was the one who first made the claim, and he has the credentials to back it up. . . . He is the only virgin-born, miracle-working, sinless, resurrected Son of God! You may not like the idea of Jesus being the only way, but if he truly is the Son of God and said he was the only way to salvation—can you afford to ignore his claim?[75]

CHAPTER FIVE

THE QUESTION OF AN AFTERLIFE

I am not going to try to convince you that there is an afterlife, and I am not going to present evidence of an afterlife. Instead, I am going to tell you stories of two individuals who said they visited the afterlife and let their words speak for themselves. I encourage you to read their stories to completion with an open mind.

Note: If their stories clash with your worldview, I encourage you to consider the possibility that your worldview might be wrong. Believe me, I know the feeling that accompanies this thought. It is very disorienting and unsettling; it feels as though the ground has been pulled out from underneath you (more on that in chapter seven).

The first story is that of a neuroscientist, Dr. Eben Alexander, who at the age of fifty-four visited the afterlife while in a coma. The second story is that of Colton Burpo, a three-year ten-month-old boy who also visited the afterlife, which he called heaven, while undergoing surgery.

Story #1

In November 2008 Dr. Alexander suddenly became extremely ill and was taken to Lynchburg General Hospital in Virginia. The emergency room doctor knew almost immediately that Dr. Alexander was suffering from some kind of brain infection. After undergoing many tests in the ER, he was diagnosed with severe E. coli bacterial meningitis. Throughout the testing process, he declined rapidly and was put on a ventilator to keep him breathing. He then slipped into a coma and was moved to the Medical Intensive Care Unit. He remained in a coma for seven days. While in that coma he visited the afterlife.

Backstory in Dr. Alexander's words

As much as I'd grown up wanting to believe in God and Heaven and an afterlife, my decades in the rigorous scientific world of academic neurosurgery had profoundly called into question how such things could exist. Modern neuroscience dictates that the brain gives rise to consciousness—to the mind, to the soul, to the spirit, to whatever you choose to call that invisible, intangible part of us that truly makes us who we are—and I had little doubt that it was correct. . . . Not that I was opposed to supernatural beliefs. . . . The older I got, however, the less likely that seemed. Like an ocean wearing away a beach, over the years my scientific worldview gently but steadily undermined my ability to believe in something larger.[76]

As a neurosurgeon, I'd heard many stories over the years of people who had strange experiences, usually after suffering cardiac arrest: stories of traveling to mysterious, wonderful landscapes; of talking to dead relatives—even of meeting God Himself. Wonderful stuff, no question. But all of it, in my opinion, was pure fantasy. What caused the other worldly types of experiences that such people so often report? I didn't claim to know, but I did know that they were brain based. All of consciousness is. If you don't have a working brain, you can't be conscious. This is because the brain is the machine that produces consciousness in the first place. When the machine breaks down, consciousness stops. As vastly complicated and mysterious as the actual mechanics of brain processes are, in essence the matter is as simple as that. Pull the plug and the TV goes dead. The show is over, no matter how much you might have been enjoying it. Or so I would have told you before my own brain crashed. During my coma my brain wasn't working improperly—it wasn't working *at all.* . . . I was encountering the reality of a world of consciousness that existed *completely free of the limitations of my physical brain.* . . .

As a practicing neurosurgeon with decades of research and hands-on work in the operating room behind me, I was in a better-than-average position to judge not only the reality but also the *implications* of what happened to me. . . . My experience showed me that the death of the body and the brain are not the end of consciousness, that human experience continues beyond the grave. More important, it continues under the gaze of a God who loves and cares about each one of us and about where the universe itself and all the beings within it are ultimately going.

The place I went was real.[77]

Dr. Alexander's journey

I can't say exactly when it happened, but at a certain point I became aware of some objects around me. They were a little like roots, and a little like blood vessels in a vast, muddy womb. Glowing a dark, dirty red, they reached down from some place far above to some other place equally far below. In retrospect, looking at them was like being a mole or earthworm, buried deep in the ground yet somehow able to see the tangled matrixes of roots and trees surrounding it . . . My consciousness wasn't foggy or distorted when I was there. It was just . . . *limited*. I wasn't human while I was in this place. I wasn't even animal. I was something before, and below, all that. I was simply a lone point of awareness in a timeless red-brown sea. The longer I stayed in this place, the less comfortable I became. At first I was so deeply immersed in it that there was no difference between "me" and the half-creepy, half-familiar element that surrounded me. But gradually this sense of deep, timeless, and boundaryless immersion gave way to something else: a feeling like I wasn't really part of this subterranean world at all, but trapped in it.[78]

Then I became aware of a smell: a little like feces, a little like blood, and a little like vomit. A *biological* smell, in other words, but of biological death, not of biological life. As my awareness sharpened more and more, I edged ever closer to panic. Whoever or whatever I was, I did not belong here. I needed to get out. But where would I go? Even as I asked that question, something new emerged from the darkness above: something that wasn't cold, or dead, or dark, but the exact opposite of all those things.[79]

Something had appeared in the darkness. Turning slowly, it radiated fine filaments of white-gold light, and as it did so the darkness around me began to splinter and break apart. Then I heard a new sound: a *living* sound, like the richest, most complex, most beautiful piece of music you've ever heard. Growing in volume as a pure white light descended, it obliterated the monotonous mechanical pounding that, seemingly for eons, had been my only company up until then. The light got closer and closer, spinning around and around and generating those filaments of pure white light that I now saw were tinged, here and there, with hints of gold. Then, at the very center of the light, something else appeared. I focused my awareness, hard, trying to figure out what it was. An opening. I was no longer looking *at* the slowly spinning light at all, but *through* it. The moment I understood this, I began to move up. Fast. There was a whooshing sound, and in a flash I went through the opening and found myself in a completely new world. The strangest, most beautiful world I'd ever seen.

Brilliant, vibrant, ecstatic, stunning. . . . I could heap on one adjective after another to describe what this world looked and felt like, but they'd all fall short. I felt like I was being born. Not reborn, or born again. Just born. Below me there was countryside. It was green, lush, and earthlike. It *was* earth . . . but at the same time it wasn't. It was like when your parents take you back to a place where you spent some years as a very young child. You don't know the place. Or at least you think you don't. But as you look around, something pulls at you, and you realize that a part of yourself—a part way, deep down—does remember the place after all, and is rejoicing at being back there again.

I was flying, passing over trees and fields, streams and waterfalls, and here and there, people. There were children, too, laughing and playing. The people sang and danced around in circles. And sometimes I'd see a dog, running and jumping among them, as full of joy as the people were. They wore simple yet beautiful clothes, and it seemed to me that the colors of these clothes had the same kind of living warmth as the trees and the flowers that bloomed and blossomed in the countryside around them. A beautiful, incredible dream world. . . . Except it wasn't a dream. Though I didn't know where I was or even *what* I was, I was absolutely sure of one thing: this place I'd suddenly found myself in was completely real.[80]

I was in a place of clouds. Big, puffy, pink-white ones that showed up sharply against the deep blue-black sky. Higher than the clouds—immeasurably higher—flocks of transparent orbs, shimmering beings arced across the sky, leaving long, streamer-like lines behind them. Birds? Angels? . . . neither of these words do justice to the beings themselves, which were quite simply different from anything I have known on this planet. They were more advanced. *Higher.* A sound, huge and booming like a glorious chant, came down from above, and I wondered if the winged beings were producing it. . . . The sound was palpable and almost material, like a rain that you can feel on your skin but that doesn't get you wet.

Seeing and hearing were not separate in this place where I now was. I could *hear* the visual beauty of the silvery bodies of those scintillating beings above, and I could see the surging, joyful perfection of what they sang. It seemed that you could not look at or listen to anything in this world without becoming a part of it—without joining with it in some mysterious way.... A warm wind blew through, like the kind that spring up on the most perfect summer days, tossing the leaves of the trees and flowing past like heavenly water. A divine breeze. It changed everything, shifting the world around me into an even higher octave, a higher vibration.

Although I still had little language function, at least as we think of it on earth, I began wordlessly putting questions to this wind—and to the divine being that I sensed at work behind or within it. *Where is this place? Who am I? Why am I here?* Each time I silently posed one of these questions, the answer came instantly in an explosion of light, color, love, and beauty that blew through me like a crashing wave. What was important about these bursts was that they didn't simply silence my questions by overwhelming them. They *answered* them, but in a way that bypassed language. Thoughts entered me directly. But it wasn't thought like we experience on earth. It wasn't vague, immaterial, or abstract. These thoughts were solid and immediate—hotter than fire and wetter than water—and as I received them I was able to instantly and effortlessly understand concepts that would have taken me years to fully grasp in my earthly life.

I continued moving forward and found myself entering an immense void, completely dark, infinite in size, yet also infinitely comforting. Pitch black as it was, it was also brimming over with light: a light that seemed to come from a brilliant orb that I now sensed near me. An orb that was living and almost solid, as the songs of the angel beings had been.

My situation was, strangely enough, something akin to that of a fetus in a womb. The fetus floats in the womb with the silent partner of the placenta, which nourishes it and mediates its relationship to the everywhere present yet at the same time invisible mother. In this case, the "mother" was God, the Creator, the Source who is responsible for making the universe and all in it. This Being was so close that there seemed to be no distance at all between God and myself. Yet at the same time, I could sense the infinite vastness of the Creator, could see how completely miniscule I was by comparison. I will occasionally use *Om* as the pronoun for God because I originally used that name in my writings after my coma. "Om" was the sound I remembered hearing associated with that omniscient, omnipotent, and unconditionally loving God, but any descriptive word falls short.

The pure vastness separating Om and me was, I realized, why I had the Orb as my companion. In some manner I couldn't completely comprehend but was sure of nonetheless, the Orb was a kind of "interpreter" between me and this extraordinary presence surrounding me. It was as if I were being born into a larger world, and the universe itself was like a giant cosmic womb, and the Orb . . . was guiding me through this process.[81]

Through the Orb, Om told me that there is not one universe but many—in fact, more than I could conceive— but that love lay at the center of them all. Evil was present in all the other universes as well, but only in the tiniest trace amounts. Evil was necessary because without it free will was impossible, and without free will there could be no growth—no forward movement, no chance for us to become what God longed for us to be. Horrible and all-powerful as evil sometimes seemed to be in a world like ours, in the larger picture love was overwhelmingly dominant, and would ultimately be triumphant.[82]

Love is, without a doubt, the basis of everything. . . . In its purest and most powerful form, this love is not jealous or selfish, but *unconditional*. This is the reality of realities, the incomprehensible truth of truths that lives and breathes at the core of everything that exists or that ever will exist, and no remotely accurate understanding of who and what we are can be achieved by anyone who does not know it, and embody it in all of their actions. . . .[83]

I understood—in the wordless way I understood everything then—that I was no longer of this place, but only visiting it. . . . This whole adventure, it began to occur to me, was some kind of tour—some kind of grand overview of the invisible, spiritual side of existence.[84]

I moved down through great walls of clouds. There was murmuring all around me, but I couldn't understand the words. Then I realized that countless beings were surrounding me, kneeling in arcs that spread into the distance. . . . They were praying for me. . . . I was on my way back, but I was not alone—and I knew I'd never feel alone again.[85]

I didn't make it back to church until December 2008. . . . At last, I understood what religion was really all about. Or at least was supposed to be about. I didn't just believe in God; I knew God. As I hobbled to the altar to take Communion, tears streamed down my cheeks.[86]

Colton's story

Colton Burpo's appendix burst in March 2003. His abdominal pain was initially misdiagnosed. By the time it was correctly diagnosed, poison had been seeping into his body for five days, and he was near death. He then underwent two surgeries to clean the poison out of him. During one of these surgeries, he visited heaven.

The first his parents became aware of his supernatural experience was the following July when his mother asked him if he remembered being in the hospital. "Yes, Mommy, I remember," he said. "That's where the angels sang to me."[87]

Once his parents, Todd and Sonja Burpo, somewhat recovered their composure, the following conversation ensued, beginning with his father stating,

> "Colton, you said that angels sang to you while you were at the hospital?" He nodded his head vigorously. "What did they sing to you?" Colton turned his eyes up and to the right, the attitude of remembering. "Well, they sang 'Jesus loves me' and 'Joshua Fought the Battle of Jericho,'" he said earnestly. "I asked them to sing 'We Will, We Will Rock You,' but they wouldn't sing that.". . . Colton's answer had been quick and matter-of-fact, without a hint of hesitation.[88]

Todd then asked him what the angels looked like, and the conversation continued.

> "Well, one of them looked like Grandpa Dennis, but it wasn't him, 'cause Grandpa Dennis has

glasses." Then he grew serious. "Dad, Jesus had the angels sing to me because I was so scared. They made me feel better." . . . "You mean Jesus was there?" "Yeah, Jesus was there." "Well, where was Jesus?". . . "I was sitting in Jesus' lap."[89]

When his parents once again recovered their composure, the conversation again continued, beginning with Todd asking Colton where he was when he saw Jesus. Colton answered,

> "Well, at the hospital. You know, when Dr. O'Holleran was working on me." "Well, Dr. O'Holleran worked on you a couple of times, remember?". . . "Are you sure it was at the hospital?" . . . "Yeah, at the hospital. When I was with Jesus, you were praying, and Mommy was talking on the phone.". . . "But you were in the operating room, Colton. How could you know what we were doing?" "Cause I could see you. I went up out of my body and I was looking down and I could see the doctor working on my body. And I saw you and Mommy. You were in a little room by yourself, praying; and Mommy was in a different room, and she was praying and talking on the phone."[90]

About one week later Todd and Colton had another conversation about Colton's experience. Todd initiated it by asking Colton if he remembered talking about sitting on Jesus' lap. When Colton replied that he did, Todd went on to ask him if anything else happened. Colton replied

"Did you know that Jesus has a cousin? Jesus told me his cousin baptized him"..."I don't remember his name, but he was really nice."[91]

As Todd was trying to sort out his reaction to these statements, Colton spontaneously said, "Hey, Dad, did you know Jesus has a horse?" "A horse?" "Yeah, a rainbow horse. I got to pet him. There's lots of colors"... "Where are there lots of colors, Colton?" "In heaven, Dad. That's where all the rainbow colors are."... "You were in heaven?" "Well, yeah, Dad."[92]

After Todd took a break to process this new information and talk to Sonja, he resumed the conversation with Colton.

> "What did Jesus look like?"..."Jesus has markers."
> "What?" "Markers, Daddy.... Jesus has markers.
> And he has brown hair and he has hair on his
> face."... "And his eyes... Oh Dad, his eyes are
> so pretty!"... "What about his clothes?"... "He
> had purple on.... His clothes were white, but it
> was purple from here to here." [moving his hand
> from his left shoulder to his right hip] "Jesus was
> the only one in heaven who had purple on, Dad.
> Did you know that?"... "And he had this gold
> thing on his head." He put both hands on his
> head in the shape of a circle.... "Colton, you
> said Jesus had markers. You mean like markers
> that you color with?" "Yeah, like colors. He had
> colors on him." "Like when you color a page?"
> "Yeah." "Well, what color are Jesus' markers?"
> "Red, Daddy. Jesus has red markers on him."...

"Colton, where are Jesus' markers?" Without hesitation, he stood to his feet. He held out his right hand, palm up and pointed to the center of it with his left. Then he held out his left palm and pointed with his right hand. Finally, Colton bent over and pointed to the tops of both his feet. "That's where Jesus' markers are, Daddy."[93]

A few days later Todd picked up the conversation with Colton once again.

"Remember when you were telling me what Jesus looks like? And about the horse?" He nodded, eyes wide and earnest. "You were in heaven?" He nodded again. . . . "Well, what did you do in heaven? " . . . "Homework." . . . "What do you mean?" Colton smiled. "Jesus was my teacher." "Like school?" "Jesus gave me work to do, and that was my favorite part of heaven. There were lots of kids, Dad." . . . "So what did the kids look like? What do people look like in heaven?" "Everybody's got wings." . . . "Did you have wings?" . . . "Yeah, but mine weren't very big." . . . "Okay . . . did you walk places or did you fly?" "We flew. Well, all except for Jesus. He was the only one in heaven who didn't have wings. Jesus just went up and down like an elevator." . . . "Everyone kind of looks like angels in heaven, Dad." "What do you mean?" "All the people have a light above their head." . . . "A light, huh?" "Yeah, and they have yellow from here to here," [making the sash motion again] "And white from here to here." He placed his hands on his shoulders, then bent forward and touched the tops of his feet.[94]

Soon after this Colton spontaneously said to his father, "Daddy, remember when I yelled for you in the hospital when I waked up?" . . . "Of course I do." . . . "Well, the reason I was yelling was that Jesus came to get me. He said I had to go back because he was answering your prayer. That's how come I was yelling for you."[95]

Then, in August, while riding in his dad's truck with Todd, Colton spontaneously said,

> "Dad, you had a grandpa named Pop, didn't you?" "Yep, sure did." . . . "Was he your mommy's daddy or your daddy's daddy?" "Pop was my mom's dad. He passed away when I was not much older than you." Colton smiled. "He's really nice." . . . "So you saw Pop?" "Yeah, I got to stay with him in heaven." . . . "Colton, what did Pop look like?" He broke into a big grin. "Oh, Dad, Pop has really big wings."[96]

One evening in October Colton interrupted Sonja while she was doing some paperwork and said,

> "Mommy, I have two sisters." . . . "No, you have your sister, Cassie, and . . . do you mean your cousin, Traci?" "No, I have two *sisters*. You had a

baby die in your tummy, didn't you?" . . . "Who told you I had a baby die in my tummy?" . . . "She did, Mommy. She said she died in your tummy." . . . "She's okay. God adopted her." . . . "Don't you mean Jesus adopted her?" . . . "No, Mommy. His Dad did!" . . . "So what did she look like?" . . . She looked a lot like Cassie. . . . She is just a little bit smaller, and she has dark hair." . . . "In heaven, this little girl ran up to me, and she wouldn't stop hugging me." . . . "What was her name? What was the little girl's name?" . . . She doesn't have a name. You guys didn't name her." . . . "You're right. Colton. We didn't even know she was a she." . . . "Yeah, she said she just can't wait for you and Daddy to get to heaven."[97]

In December, after reading Colton a bedtime story about King Solomon, Todd initiated another conversation with Colton about his visit to heaven.

"When you were in heaven, did you ever see God's throne?" . . . "What's a throne, Daddy?" I picked up the Bible storybook and pointed to the picture of Solomon seated in his court. "A throne is like the king's chair. It's the chair that only the king can sit in." "Oh, yeah! I saw that a bunch of times!" . . . "Well, what did God's throne look like?" "It was big, Dad . . . *really, really* big, because God is the biggest one there is. And he really, really loves us, Dad. You can't *belieeeeve* how much he loves us!" . . . "And do you know that Jesus sits right next to God?" Colton went on excitedly. "Jesus' chair is right next to his Dad's!" . . . "Colton, which side of God's throne was Jesus sitting on?" Colton climbed up on the bed and faced me on his knees. "Well, pretend like you're in God's throne. Jesus sat right there," he said, pointing to my right side. . . . "Well, who sits on the other side of God's throne?" "Oh, that's easy, Dad. That's where the angel Gabriel is. He's really nice." . . . "Where did you sit, Colton?" "They brought in a little chair for me, I sat by God the Holy Spirit. Did you know that God is three persons, Dad?" "Yeah, I think I know that one." "I was sitting by God the Holy Spirit because I was praying for you. You needed the Holy Spirit, so I prayed for you."[98]

Todd's words

For months in late 2003 and early 2004, there was a certain set of things that Colton seemed to fixate on. He talked about death and dying more weird—*really* weird—for a kid his age. He also shared more about what heaven looks like. These details came out in bits and pieces over dinner, while he ran errands with Sonja and me, and during the general flow of life. . . . No matter what new tidbits he revealed, though, Colton had one consistent theme: he talked constantly about how much Jesus loves the children. I mean that: *constantly.*[99]

During that time, Colton had also become obsessed with rainbows. . . . So when, in the spring of 2004, the most brilliant rainbow we'd ever seen appeared . . . we called him outside to take a look. . . . He emerged from the playroom and joined us on the front stoop. "Look at that rainbow, Colton," Sonja said. "There definitely should be a big pot of gold at the end of that thing." Colton squinted, peering up at colors pouring across the sky. "Cool," he said with a nonchalant smile. I prayed for that yesterday." Then he turned on his heel and went back to play. . . . Colton Burpo hadn't seen a rainbow in a while, so he asked his heavenly Father to send one.[100]

My words

I would like to close this chapter by reiterating Colton's words to his father in December 2003: "God is the biggest one there is. And he really, really loves us, Dad. You can't *belieeeeve* how much he loves us!"

CHAPTER SIX

IS THE BIBLE TRUSTWORTHY?

Since the story of God's relationship with the human race is told in the Bible, it is important that one can trust that the Bible is a factual account of actual occurrences and real people's lives, not a myth, a legend, or a fictitious story. Even further, it is super important that one can trust that the four Gospels tell the accurate story of a real person, Jesus Christ.

"If the Jesus of faith is not also the Jesus of history, he's powerless and he's meaningless. Unless he's rooted in reality, unless he established his divinity by rising from the dead, he's just a feel-good symbol who's as irrelevant as Santa Claus. But there's good evidence that he's more than that."[101]

"There are specific tests that scholars, researchers, and archaeologists use to determine the authenticity of a historical document. These are the bibliographical test, the internal evidence test, and the external evidence test."[102]

Bibliographical test

"The bibliographical test is an examination of the textual transmission by which documents reach us."[103]

> As with other documents of ancient literature, there are no known extant original manuscripts of the Bible. Fortunately, however, the abundance of manuscript copies makes it possible to reconstruct the original text with virtually complete accuracy. . . . The authenticity of the New Testament text we have today rests on a foundation of a massive amount of historical documentation. . . . Without question, the New Testament boasts the best-attested manuscript transmission when compared with other ancient documents. The bibliographical test validates and confirms that the New Testament has been accurately transmitted to us through the centuries.[104]

In summary, "Scholars representing different types of expertise and different eras agree that the text of the New Testament meets the first bibliographic test."[105]

Internal evidence test

The bibliographical test indicates that the New Testament as it has come down to us through the ages is what the original authors of the four Gospels and the letters actually wrote. The internal evidence test determined that what they wrote is a true and accurate account of Jesus's life and ministry.

In an interview with Lee Strobel, Craig Blomberg, who is "widely considered to be one of the country's foremost authorities on the biographies of Jesus,"[106] stated,

> It's important to acknowledge that strictly speaking, the gospels are anonymous. But the uniform testimony of the early church was that Matthew, also known as Levi, the tax collector and one of the twelve disciples, was the author of the first gospel in the New Testament; that John Mark, a companion of Peter, was the author of the gospel we call Mark; and that Luke, known as Paul's "beloved physician," wrote both the gospel of Luke and the Acts of the Apostles. . . . The rest of the early testimony is unanimous that it was John the apostle—the son of Zebedee—who wrote the [fourth] gospel."[107]

In *Evidence That Demands a Verdict*, the McDowells go on to state that it "can be reasonably argued that all four biographies of Jesus in the New Testament, as well as the book of Acts, were written within a few decades—and certainly within a century—of the events they describe."[108] Therefore, if you accept that Blomberg is accurately reporting who the authors of the Gospels are, and the McDowells are accurately reporting time frames for when the Gospels were written, it is not much of a leap to believe that direct or indirect eyewitness testimonies and oral histories were the basis of their accounts.

Now I realize that, although in our day and age eyewitness testimony and oral histories are not necessarily considered to be foolproof, the same does not hold true for the first-century Jewish culture:

> There is a popular tendency to believe the disciples of Jesus were mere peasants from Galilee, illiterate fisherman, who had received no education. Scholars, in fact, had often begun with the biased assumption that the apostles could not possibly have written what was traditionally attributed to them, so that much of the gospel had to have been drawn from the imagination of later writers more gifted and more educated than they.
>
> This bias could not be further from the truth. The disciples were not illiterate. Though, by the first century, the Jews spoke Aramaic, they nevertheless wrote in a common Greek dialect known as *koine* and knew how to read and write Hebrew. They were grounded in the tradition of accurate memorization of oral instruction. The Jews were the most literate people in the world. While it would be impossible for us today to hear a speech or a sermon and later retell it accurately to others, it would not have been difficult for first-century Jews, who had been schooled in this ability from early childhood. In fact, their level of education would not be matched until Britain and the United States developed the public school system in the late eighteen hundreds.[109]

The Jewish school system

After their return from the Babylonian exile, the Jews began to create what we could recognize as learning centers. . . . These houses of study . . . were used for worship and for the exposition of Scripture on the Sabbath for the edification of adults but also became centers for the education of Jewish boys. An important part of this education was the memorization of Scripture. . . . Because the Torah was written in Hebrew, the children were required to learn that language as well as to become literate in their native tongue, Aramaic. . . . This degree of textual precision imparted to the nation's youth should lead one to be much more cautious about questioning the accuracy of the reporting of the words and actions of Jesus in the New Testament. Most particularly, one should appreciate the faithfulness of the Jewish recorders in documenting such an extremely important subject as Jesus. They would not have been accustomed to playing fast and loose with the facts or to exaggerating their descriptions of events. Their lifelong training would have resulted in a precision with words as well as thoughts. To disregard this aspect of Jewish education, and to treat the gospel record as filled with hyperbole and fanciful legends, would be a serious error.[110]

Further, "at the time the gospels were written there were still numerous well-known living eyewitnesses to Jesus's teaching and life events. They had committed them to memory and they remained active in the public life of the churches throughout their lifetimes, serving as ongoing sources and guarantors of the truth of those accounts."[111]

Timothy Keller, in *The Reason for God*, presents further evidence that the Gospels are true and accurate accounts of events that occurred in Jesus's ministry:

Richard Bauckham has compiled a great deal of research by psychologists on the marks of recollective memory. He looks at the marks of eyewitness accounts of events and how they differ from speculative or fictional accounts, or of composite historical reconstructions. Recollective memory is selective—it fixes on unique and consequential events, it retains irrelevant detail, it takes the limited vantage point of a participant rather than that of an omniscient narrator, and it shows signs of frequent rehearsal. Bauckham then shows these same marks in the gospel narratives. Vivid and important events can stay with you for decades if frequently rehearsed and/or retold. Factor in the fact that disciples in the ancient world were expected to memorize masters' teachings, and that many of Jesus's statements are presented in a form that was actually designed for memorization, and you have every reason to trust the accounts.[112]

External evidence test

External evidence tests, as the name suggests, examine non-biblical sources and documents to see if they corroborate the content of the Bible.

> As a young scholar, I [Josh] asked the question: *how can I prove that Christianity is false?* I traveled to many libraries in the US and in Europe in my search to find the answer. After trying to shatter the historicity, validity, and authenticity of the Scriptures, I came to the conclusion that the Bible is historically trustworthy.[113]

Though there are numerous Christian writers, primarily leaders of the early church, who corroborate the Bible's content, I am going to highlight the corroboration by some non-Christian writers.

Tacitus, a first-century Roman historian, wrote this about the great fire of Rome: "Nero fastened the guilt and inflicted the most exquisite tortures on a class hated for their abominations, called Christians by the populace. Christus, from whom the name had its origin, suffered the extreme penalty during the reign of Tiberias at the hands of one of our procurators, Pontius Pilate."[114]

Suetonius,

> chief secretary to Emperor Hadrian (who reigned from AD 117–138) . . . confirms the report in Acts 18:2 that Claudius commanded all Jews to leave Rome in AD 49 . . . Then, speaking of the

aftermath of the great fire at Rome, Suetonius reports, "Punishment was inflicted on the Christians, a body of people addicted to a novel and mischievous superstition."[115]

Josephus "was a Pharisee of the priestly line and a Jewish historian, though working under Roman authority and with some care so as not to offend the Romans."[116] He is credited with having written four manuscripts in the latter part of the first century. In his writings he mentions that the Jewish high priest Ananias ordered the stoning of James and refers to James as Jesus's brother. He also mentions John the Baptist in his writings, stating that John was killed by King Herod.

In addition, "archaeology, a relative newcomer among the physical sciences, has provided exciting and dramatic confirmation of the Bible's accuracy."[117] "Archaeology has provided information that confirms historical detail to which Luke refers in writing the gospel bearing his name."[118] Further, "thanks to many archaeological finds, most of the ancient cities mentioned in the book of Acts have been identified. The journeys of Paul can now be accurately traced as a result of these finds."[119]

Even further,

In his epistle to the Romans, written from Corinth, Paul makes mention of the city treasurer, Erastus ["Erastus, the city treasurer, sends you his greetings" Romans 16:23]. During the excavations of Corinth in 1929, a pavement was found inscribed: ERASTVS PRO:AED:S:P:STRAVIT

(Erastus, curator of public buildings, laid this pavement at his own expense) . . . The pavement quite likely existed in the first century AD, and the donor and the man Paul mentions are probably one and the same. . . . Also found in Corinth is a fragmentary inscription believed to have borne the words *Synagogue of the Hebrews.* Conceivably it stood over the doorway of the synagogue where Paul debated ["Each Sabbath found Paul at the synagogue, trying to convince the Jews and Greeks alike." Acts 18:4].[120]

Finally, three of the four Gospels speak of darkness descending on the earth during the last few hours of Jesus's life. "At noon, darkness fell across the whole land until three o'clock" (Matthew 27:45). Mark's Gospel contains these exact words in Mark 15:33, and Luke's Gospel reports, "By this time it was about noon, and darkness fell across the whole land until three o'clock" (Luke 23:44). This was corroborated in AD 52 by Thallus, a historian. He "wrote a history of the eastern Mediterranean world since the Trojan War. Although Thallus's work has been lost, it was quoted by Julius Africanus in about AD 221—and it made reference to the darkness that the gospels had written about!"[121]

A word about the Old Testament

Before I close out this chapter, I wish to address the authenticity of the book of Exodus in the Old Testament, as I discussed the Jews' exodus from Egypt in chapters three and four.

Though there is little to no external written evidence to validate the exodus of the Jewish people from Egypt as an actual historical event, there is massive internal evidence that does so.

In regard to the lack of external written evidence, the McDowells state that

> Egyptians might never have written about the Hebrews. Richard Freund has studied ancient Egypt for many years and has become convinced "that they [Egyptians], like the Stalinist regime of the former Soviet Union, were concerned with controlling the information flow, had an overarching perspective on their cumulative history, and were indeed experts on public relations. I cannot imagine that they would have advertised in their written or pictorial history their need to enslave anyone to create the marvelous institutions of Egypt."[122]

They also state, "Biblical theologian John Sailhamer acknowledges the lack of clear Egyptian evidence. . . . 'No Egyptian records describe the Exodus. One would not expect such an account. The primary purpose of Egyptian records at that period was to cast pharaoh in a positive light, and the events of the biblical narrative would do anything but that.'"[123]

There is, however, some archeological evidence.

> Archaeologists almost universally believe a city discovered at Qantir is ancient Pi-Ramesses. . . . This ancient royal residence would correspond to

the biblical Rameses. If so, then this would mean Israel began the exodus from this city. From here, the most natural route seems like it would have been to head north via an already established road to Canaan. . . . But Israel did not take this most obvious route. Exodus 13:17 says, "When Pharaoh let the people go, God did not lead them by way of the land of the Philistines, although that was near" (ESV). . . .The reason God led Israel southeast instead of by the expected northern route is explained in Exodus 13:17: "For God said, 'Lest the people change their minds when they see war and return to Egypt'" (ESV). Archaeological discoveries have shown fortifications that lead researchers to conclude that following the northern road to Canaan would have indeed subjected Israel to war, which confirms the Exodus account of why they avoided it.[124]

In regard to internal evidence, the exodus of the Israelites from Egypt is mentioned and referenced throughout both the Old and the New Testaments. (See Appendix One.) Also, "the Bible presents the exodus as a historical event. . . . The narrative tells us of specific people . . . places . . . and events,"[125] and "the history of Israel is dated from the Passover, just as the United States is dated from the Declaration of Independence."[126] For those not familiar with the story of the Passover, see Appendix Two.

CHAPTER SEVEN

MY STORY: FROM RELIGION TO RELATIONSHIP

I grew up in suburban New York City as the oldest of four children in an Irish Catholic family. From the outside we looked like a normal, happy family. Both biological parents were present, we always had food, clothes, and shelter; there was no physical or sexual abuse; we went to church and school; and we had strong ties to extended family. In spite of all of this, though, I grew up feeling alone and disconnected from others in my family and from people in general.

I attribute my feelings of aloneness and disconnection to the fact that my family never talked about anything personal. I don't recall either of my parents ever asking me how I was or how my day was going. Though we tended to have very lively, and sometimes rather loud, discussions around the dinner table, the discussions almost always revolved around politics, sports, and world events. Opinions were debated. Feelings were never shared. What went on inside each of us on an emotional, human level was never acknowledged or even mentioned. No one taught me that it was okay to have feelings and needs or that it was okay to talk about them. This resulted in my feelings becoming like foreign objects to me. I was totally unaware of them, totally cut off from them. The secondary result was that I did not have the faintest clue how to connect with anyone in a real, authentic way.

Two lessons I learned growing up in my family (lessons that, of course, I didn't realize at the time that I was learning them) were:

1. Other people's opinions were very important, and I needed to please others and do whatever I could to gain people's approval.
2. I needed to earn self-worth and love through what I did. The idea that I could be loved and valued just for who I was, separate from what I did, was completely off my radar, totally outside my frame of reference. The paths to earning love, acceptance, worth, and value that I found, or that were laid out for me, were academic achievement and taking care of people.

I subsequently grew into an approval seeker, people pleaser, and overachiever par excellence! I was filled with a desperate drivenness to always "do," accompanied by chronic feelings of inadequacy. No matter what I did, how much I did, or how well I did it, it was never enough, or so I thought. The image I had in my mind of what I thought I should be, compared to my picture of what I thought I was, taunted me constantly. It was the fuel that powered my dysfunctional, performance-based patterns of overachieving.

While I was learning at home that I had to earn my parents' love and acceptance by what I did, I was learning in church (Catholic) and in school (Catholic) that I also had to earn God's love and earn my way into heaven. I learned that where I spent eternity would be determined by what I did (good works), along with where I was in the Catholic check-and-balance system when I died.

The check-and–balance system

I learned that certain types and amounts of good works and penance make up for certain sins and that sins are divided into the categories of venial and mortal. I learned that if I die with mortal sins on my soul that I have not sufficiently made up for with good works and penance, I will spend time suffering in purgatory to purge my soul of these sins. The amount of time I will spend in purgatory will depend on where I am in the check-and-balance system regarding sins and good deeds at the time of my death.

My picture of God was of a very cold, distant, critical deity who didn't care about how I felt or what I needed and who had very high expectations of me—so high that it was doubtful I would ever reach them—and who wouldn't love me or welcome me into heaven unless I achieved them. He certainly was not someone I could trust or depend on. He was someone to be afraid of and stay away from. Not surprisingly, I drifted away from church and God in my early adulthood. I didn't miss anything because church to me was performing empty rituals and reciting memorized responses and prayers that I didn't understand, and God was just one more person who, no matter what I did or how much I did, I would never be able to please. This greatly added to my sense of not being able to measure up no matter how hard I tried, and it caused me to be afraid not only of life on earth but also of life in the hereafter.

A direction for my life

When I was a senior in high school, I took a psychology course and became fascinated with the concept that there are reasons people do what they do and feel what they feel. I subsequently majored in psychology in college; went to graduate school, where I earned a master's degree in clinical social work; and embarked on a career as a psychotherapist. I also entered therapy myself due to feeling chronically depressed. I was unhappy and I didn't know why, and I didn't have the first clue how to change it.

I soon began to realize that I had been wounded in childhood. I had thought my family and childhood were okay due to the factors I have listed above. I was so used to feeling alone, disconnected, and not as good as others that I just assumed these feelings were normal. The thought that maybe something was wrong with my family never entered my consciousness or found its way onto my radar screen. As I began to understand what had happened in my family, and as the unspoken rules my family lived by became clear to me, I slowly came to understand that I had been emotionally neglected. I was then able to identify some of the unhealthy thought and behavior patterns I habitually engaged in and change them to healthier ones.

A few years into my career I got married and eventually became the mother of two children. It was my children who brought me back to church and eventually to God. It was important to me that my children develop good moral values, and I figured that the best way to make this happen was to raise them in a church, though I knew I did not want to raise them in the Catholic Church. So, not long after my second child was born, I started to look around for a church to join. As my husband had grown up in a United Methodist church, we settled on a local United Methodist church and started attending regularly.

At first I was going for the kids, though it wasn't long before I started going for myself. I started hearing that Christ died for me and that God wanted a personal relationship with me. Those were totally foreign concepts to me and very difficult to wrap my mind around. What really blew my mind, though, was learning in a Bible study that there is no such thing as purgatory. That brought into question everything I had been taught growing up. On top of that, I learned in a subsequent Bible study that I could not earn God's love. Out of a twelve-week Bible study the only thing I retained was the following phrase: "Don't just do something. Stand there!"[127] As a task-oriented individual who had historically functioned as an overachiever, just being and not doing went against my grain on a very deep level. I just could not imagine how anyone could love me if I wasn't doing something to please them or gain their approval.

As I stated at the beginning of chapter five, I know how disorienting and unsettling it is when beliefs you hold are challenged and/or proven to be untrue. It feels as though the ground is being pulled out from underneath you. This is how I felt when I learned that there is no such thing as purgatory and that it is impossible to earn God's love. So, I began questioning everything I had been taught about God, searching for truth and deciding what I believed and didn't believe. I eventually came to the conclusion that the God of my childhood is not the real God.

I began to believe that God really does love me and care about how I feel and what I need and that he will take care of me and provide for me. I spent months reading Matthew 6:25–33 (see Appendix Three) every day, and I slowly began to believe that if God takes care of the birds and the flowers he will take care of me. I began to understand that he wants to be involved in my life day to day, minute by minute (not just for an hour on Sunday morning) and that he loves me so much that he sent his only Son, Jesus, to suffer and die for me; in fact, Jesus would have suffered and died even if I had been the only person on the planet! I finally understood and believed that God wants me to have a relationship with Jesus and to follow Jesus, not a bunch of manmade rules, such as whether or not I eat meat on Friday. And I finally understood that there was nothing I could do to earn my way to heaven. When he died on the cross and rose again, victorious over death and the grave, Jesus offered me the gift of spending eternity in heaven with him. I could choose either to accept or not to accept his free gift. I chose to accept it and started to walk with him.

Growing the relationship

Any relationship, if it is to be healthy and vibrant, needs to be nurtured. This is true not only for our human relationships but also for our relationship with God. We nurture and grow our relationship with God through prayer.

As a child, my experience with prayer had been reciting memorized prayers that someone else had written for use during specified times in liturgies. As these prayers were never explained to me, I had no understanding of what the words and phrases meant that I was reciting. Prayer was empty and meaningless to me.

As my relationship with God grew and developed, though, I began to see prayer in a new and different light. I began to see it as a relational dialogue. I could talk to the God of the universe, and he talked to me! What an awesome privilege! It took me a while, though, to recognize his voice. Over time I came to understand that he communicated with me in a variety of ways, one of which was not audible words. Sometimes he would communicate with me in the form of an internal prompting that wouldn't go away until I did whatever I was being prompted to do. Sometimes he would talk to me by having words jump off a page as I read the Bible. At other times his communication would come in the form of a strong emotional response as I was listening to a worship song. Still other times, God chose to speak to me through people.

Developing a prayer life was challenging for me. As I had not been taught in childhood that it was okay to express my feelings and needs, engaging in dialogue in which I was emotionally honest and vulnerable was scary. I struggled with this in both my human relationships and my relationship with God.

As I got to know God and understand his character, I was able to see the differences between my earthly parents and my heavenly parent. I came to realize and believe that though my earthly parents had not engaged in this kind of authentic dialogue with me, my heavenly parent was different. He wanted authentic dialogue, not superficial chatter. As I began to tell him the desires of my heart and ask him for what I truly wanted, my relationship with him became more vibrant, and he became more firmly rooted in the center of my life. An ongoing dialogue with God gradually wove itself into the very fabric of my daily life and became as automatic to me as breathing. Though I have not received everything that I have asked for, I trust that God hears me and, as a good parent, considers everything that I say and ask for and answers my prayers in the way that he deems best for me.

Walking with Jesus

Fairly early in my faith walk (mid- to late 1990s), I started experiencing a nagging sense that I was supposed to do something for God. It kept gnawing at me inside and wouldn't go away. Though I had this feeling that I was supposed to do something for God, I didn't have the faintest idea what it was I was supposed to do. In an effort to try to understand the task to which God was calling me, I served on and then led a committee in my church and also served in a number of different ministries. Though all of these were good and enjoyable and somewhat fulfilling, not one of them felt like the right fit.

In 2003 I was leading a group in my church's Small Group Ministry. In spring/early summer of that year a notice went out to all the small group leaders that the senior pastor was going to Saddleback Church in California to learn about a faith-based recovery program called Celebrate Recovery. The notice included an open invitation for anyone who was interested to join him. I went, and while I was there, God finally let me know what he wanted me to do for him. He let me know beyond the shadow of a doubt that he wanted me to be a Celebrate Recovery ministry leader. When we got back to Pennsylvania, the church did decide to start a Celebrate Recovery ministry, and I did become the ministry leader.

What followed was one of the most difficult years of my life. Establishing and leading the Celebrate Recovery ministry was far harder than I had ever imagined it would be. It was full of struggle, challenges, conflict, anger, hurt, fear, and self-doubt. Power battles abounded. My leadership was constantly challenged and undermined. There was a period of time in spring '04 during which I was particularly discouraged and full of doubt. One morning while I was praying, I asked God to show me what I needed to read or to hear, and I opened my Bible to 1 Chronicles 28 (David commissioning Solomon to build the temple). I started to read that chapter, and the last two verses almost jumped off the page at me: "Then David continued, 'Be strong and courageous, and do the work. Don't be afraid or discouraged by the size of the task, for the LORD God, my God, is with you. He will not fail you or forsake you. He will see to it that all the work related to the Temple of the LORD is finished correctly. The various divisions of priests and Levites will serve in the Temple of God. Others with skills of every kind will volunteer, and the officials and the entire nation are at your command.'"

This confirmed to me that God did indeed want me to be a leader. I began to read those verses every day, sometimes multiple times in one day, and I slowly began to feel the burden of weight lifted off my shoulders. I *knew* that I wasn't alone, that God was in control. All I had to do was follow his plan, and he would do the rest. As I trusted that more and more, my faith became stronger and my fear decreased. I stopped people pleasing and approval seeking, and I started to lead with more confidence and purpose. As I truly led the ministry, though, the challenges to my leadership and the power struggles intensified, until they culminated in a head-on collision with the stained-glass ceiling.

In November '04 I was removed from the position of Celebrate Recovery ministry leader by the pastors and some lay leaders in the church. I didn't see this coming and was initially in shock. When the shock lessened, I was devastated. I began a period of deep grieving and mourning. I was hurt, angry, depressed. I felt as though I were wandering in the wilderness, lost.

It's difficult to describe the depth of joy I felt at finally discovering and fulfilling God's purpose for my life. It's even more difficult to describe the depth of pain I felt at having that ripped away from me by human beings. Although I was devastated and in more emotional pain than at almost any other time in my life, I never once doubted God's call on my life. I saw my removal from the leadership of Celebrate Recovery as a human thing and not a God thing. At the same time, I also believed that it could not have happened unless God allowed it to happen.

I've heard it said that great lessons are learned in times of great pain, and that certainly proved to be true for me. During my time in the wilderness, God brought me much closer to him, teaching me to trust him, his timing, and his plan on a much deeper level. He also taught me that my source of self-esteem and self-worth is not in my professional work or in my ministry, as I had previously thought. It's in my relationship with him, and I belong to him, not to any particular church or ministry. I know that I know that I know that he will not abandon or forsake me, no matter what. I don't have to perform, achieve, take care of anyone, please others, or gain others' approval in order for God to love me. He loves me no matter what, and he knew me and loved me before he placed me in my mother's womb.

Though I immediately left my church and the ministry I had been leading, I stayed involved with the wider Celebrate Recovery ministry. I served in various roles in a few Celebrate Recovery ministries near my home until 2013, when God let me know that season of my life was over. I then spent about one year waiting on God to let me know what he wanted me to do next. I didn't have to wait long. In July 2014 God lit a fire in my heart to help his daughters be set free from belief systems and practices that reinforce the inequality of the sexes.

When God first lit that fire in my heart, I wondered whether maybe he had a sense of humor. After all, I was a woman who had been raised in a liberal Irish Catholic Democratic family in the suburbs of New York City but who was presently living in one of the most conservative, traditional counties in the United States (Lancaster County, Pennsylvania). I gradually realized, though, that as the battle for civil rights was fought in the South, where racial discrimination was the strongest, the battle for gender equality needed to be fought in a place where gender inequality is rigidly embedded. I now swim upstream against gender inequality wherever I see it. Since I see it all around me, doing this does not win me many friends, believe me. I continue to do it, though, because I believe God wants individuals to be who he created them to be and to fulfill the purposes he chose for them, rather than having roles assigned to them based on their gender.

Though I am continually challenging the rigid gender inequality I see all around me, I have no illusions that I will lead a political or social movement which will result in full gender equality. I also have no illusions that gender equality will become a reality in my lifetime. Rather, I am hoping to plant seeds for change in some hearts. I keep the following story front and center in my mind as a reminder to keep my focus clear and my goal realistic.

The Starfish Story (author unknown)
One day a man was walking along a beach when he noticed a boy picking something up and throwing it into the ocean. The man walked over to the boy and asked, "What are you doing?" The boy replied, "Throwing starfish back into the ocean. The surf is up, and the tide is going out. If I don't throw them back, they'll die." The

man said, "Son, don't you realize there are miles and miles of beach and hundreds of starfish? You can't make a difference!" The boy bent down, picked up another starfish and threw it back into the sea. Then, smiling at the man, he said, "I made a difference for that one."

CHAPTER EIGHT

BOB'S STORY: FROM ATHEIST TO BELIEVER TO PASTOR

Bob was raised as the oldest of five boys in an intact Catholic family in northern New Jersey. He received his religious education through CCD (Confraternity of Christian Doctrine) at his local church, where he made his first confession and received his first Communion in second grade. After being confirmed in seventh grade, he stopped attending CCD. He described himself as "a good Catholic boy" who "absolutely believed in God."

He began to turn away from God and toward atheism in high school, stating, "I wanted to live my life my way." His belief in atheism was cemented while attending a state university in New Jersey. In his book *Facing Life's Challenges Head On*, Bob states, "College can shake your faith, but I abandoned mine on my own. I exchanged it for all the fun that college has to offer, and I didn't cheat myself out of any of it."[128]

Bob graduated from college in 1988 with a degree in political science. After taking a year off, he went to law school in Michigan. He graduated with a law degree in 1993 and returned to New Jersey, where he opened a law firm. He took on a partner in '96. Although the firm did very well for a long time, he was never really happy. God began to change that in late 2002, when he went to work on Bob's heart. Bob describes that process in the following words:

> My wife's uncle Ken died on December 18, 2002. His death marked the start of my journey to faith. That December, I was preparing for the biggest court trial of my career, and under crushing stress. Facing about thirty lawyers who were much more experienced and better financed than I was, I knew that I was outgunned and undermanned. I had just finished a deposition in preparation for the trial and decided to go see a movie to give myself a break. As soon as I sat down in the theater my wife, Molly, called me, sobbing. "Uncle Kenny had a massive heart attack," she finally managed. I left the theater and drove home to be with her. Uncle Kenny died a few days later.[129]
>
> Uncle Kenny's funeral changed everything. It was a cold, rainy, miserable day. We stood by the graveside in the windswept rain, under umbrellas too small and puddles too big. Uncle

Kenny's teenage children, Maggie and Michael, were completely devastated by the sudden loss of their father—their hero. I will always remember Michael—who had just been selected to attend the Air Force Academy exactly forty years after his own father—splayed out on top of the casket, sobbing uncontrollably. As I saw their grief I thought, "If there is a God, why would He allow such pain and loss? Why would He allow Aunt Joan to be widowed so young and leave Maggie and Michael to grow up without their dad?" The emotion of the funeral, the stress of my upcoming trial, and the sadness of Uncle Kenny's funeral overwhelmed me. I broke down in tears and couldn't stop crying. Molly and I missed half of the gathering back at their house after the funeral because I could not regain control of myself. After we returned, I looked around at people in Molly's family who I knew had faith. I could see that they had hope while all I felt was hopelessness. They believed that though Uncle Kenny was gone, they would see him again in heaven. I wanted that hope.[130]

Over the next two years Bob read the entire New Testament, as well as several books explaining and validating Christianity. Two of those books were *The Case for Christ* by Lee Strobel and *Evidence That Demands a Verdict* by Josh McDowell. The result of his reading and reflection, in his own words: "The overwhelming weight of the evidence convinced me that Jesus Christ died, was buried, and was resurrected from the dead. I understood that He had to endure the cross to pay for my sins and that the proof that God accepted Jesus' payment for sin is that God raised Him from the dead. Because of Jesus' death and resurrection, I have eternal life. That's what it means to be a Christian, and I became one!"[131]

After accepting Jesus's gift of forgiveness for his sins and giving his life to Christ, Bob almost immediately felt himself being called into full-time ministry. Though he knew deep in his bones that this is what God wanted him to do, he was unable to fulfill this calling. Try as he might, no church would give him the opportunity for an interview. He later stated:

> In retrospect, I certainly understand. What church would hire a lawyer who's been a Christian for a month? I knew that if I were serious about being in ministry, I needed training. I also knew that I couldn't go to seminary and still afford the cost of living in New Jersey. So with my wife Molly's prayerful support, we decided that I would leave my law practice in New Jersey, we would sell our house, and move to Texas, so I could attend seminary.[132]

By the time he reached his last semester at Dallas Theological Seminary, he and Molly were financially tapped out. Though he had maintained his partnership at the law practice in New Jersey, he had not taken a paycheck in months, and the firm had a high level of debt. He and Molly had completely depleted their personal savings and had almost emptied their retirement savings accounts. The pressure he felt to find a job and earn money was intense. He had been actively looking for a ministry position, but so far nothing had materialized. Then, as he was nearing graduation, the bottom fell out of his world.

> I turned in the last two papers I would ever write in seminary. . . . About a week later, I received a voicemail from my professor saying that I cited my sources improperly, which equated to plagiarism under the seminary guidelines. He said seminary policy compelled him to fail me in the class and report me to the academic dean for further proceedings. . . . My blood ran cold. . . . Wave after wave of what-if questions flooded my brain. What if the school expels me? What if I never graduate? What if no church will hire me and I have to find another job in the legal field to pay my bills? I fell into a deep and dark depression with anxiety so severe that my body shook uncontrollably.[133]

In his book *A Leader's Heart*, John Maxwell states, "God prepares leaders in a slow-cooker, not in a microwave oven."[134] After listening to the voicemail from his professor, Bob found himself in a slow-cooker. He remained in that slow-cooker for many months.

I could barely get out of bed, move, or talk. I had no will to eat. I had virtually shut down. I even contemplated suicide. . . . I needed to see a psychologist to learn coping strategies, and a psychiatrist who could prescribe medication. . . . Mornings were the worst. I would wake up shaking like a leaf. I'd take my anxiety medicine and start counting the minutes until I could take another dose. The way my brain's chemistry worked, I tended to feel better at night. Some nights I felt like I might even be okay. But in the morning, the cycle would begin again. It was like the movie Groundhog Day. Even if I felt a little better at night, I dreaded going to sleep because I knew my anxiety would be back full throttle in the morning.[135]

Bob slowly improved due to unwavering support from Molly, the professional treatment he was receiving, prayer, and spending time in God's Word. Then,

One Sunday at Stonebriar Community Church, Steve Farrar preached a message from Psalm 71. He finished his sermon by quoting "For Your righteousness, O God, reaches to the heavens, You who have done great things; O God, who is like You? You who have shown me many troubles and distresses will revive me again" (Psalm 71:19–20 NASB1995, emphasis added). Molly and I looked at each other and fell into each other's arms crying, right there in the church service with 2000 people present. It was a stirring and moving moment I will always remember as we hoped and prayed that we could trust God's promise to revive us again.[136]

In the meantime, his professor had conferred with the powers that be at the seminary, and though Bob wasn't in the room to have firsthand knowledge of the discussion that took place, his belief is that they decided he had not cited his sources improperly on purpose. The professor gave him a passing grade, and he graduated on schedule. In addition, he began to work for a law firm in Dallas as a contract attorney on a temporary basis. He then had a reason to get out of bed in the morning and was earning money. He and Molly slowly got on their feet financially. In December 2016, Bob and his partner in the New Jersey law firm were able to pay the debts the firm had accrued and close it. He had finally simmered enough and was ready to exit the slow-cooker.

In January 2017, Bob answered an ad for a pastoral position. This resulted in his being offered and accepting the position of pastor at Grace Redeemer Community Church in Garland, Texas. He has been serving in that capacity since July 2017.

As Bob looked back on his time in the slow-cooker, he realized that God had a very special purpose for that time. "Before God allowed anxiety to crush me, I was nowhere near prepared to be a pastor. God used it to prepare me for the role that he had for me. . . . I was frustrated because I was applying for pastoral positions but receiving very few interviews. Now I know why. I was unprepared to help others because of my own brokenness."[137]

> I needed more compassion and empathy. People hire an attorney to make them financially whole. A pastor's job is to help people become spiritually whole. I was not prepared to do that . . . Seminary can't teach you compassion for people. It can't teach you to feel their pain and be willing to help. That can only come from a change to your heart and soul. Before my anxiety crisis, I would minimize or even mock other people's problems. I'd think, "Why can't you just make yourself happy? Go get an ice cream and cheer up." I had no empathy or compassion for people. Molly wasn't sure I was cut out to be a pastor. She used to pray, "God, if you are going to make him a pastor, give him a pastor's heart." God used anxiety to do it. It was only after I had experienced it, that I understood that people can't make themselves happy, and it's not shameful. We are all broken people. When my anxiety was severe, the things that I worried about might have seemed silly to anyone else. But to me they were as real as a grizzly bear. Before I could be an effective pastor, I needed to learn that other people were the same. Although I might not understand their anxiety, it was as real to them as can be. God taught me never to minimize anyone else's problems, but to have empathy and

compassion. . . . God receives all praise and glory for using a very difficult experience to prepare me for the work of shepherding and caring for His flock.[138]

God has entrusted me with a group of about 100 people who love the Lord, love His word, and strive to be more like Him every day. What a privilege it is to help to lead them where they already want to go! I'm grateful for the people that God has given me. I'm humbled that He took a sinful rebel like me, changed my heart, moved our family across the country, and gave me a ministry.[139]

AFTERWORD

I hope that by now you are, at the very least, considering the possibility that God is real; that he created the universe and everything in it; that heaven actually exists; and that Jesus suffered and died so you could spend eternity in heaven with God. I also hope you are seriously considering accepting Jesus's gift of love to you.

At the beginning of chapter one, I stated that I am not trying to convert you to a religion, and I am *still* not trying to convert you to a religion. I am encouraging you to have a personal relationship with Jesus Christ. That's what Christianity is all about. "Christianity is not a religion. Religion is humans trying to work their way to God through good works. Christianity is God coming to men and women through Jesus Christ."[140] "Christianity is not a religion. . . . It's a relationship and a lifestyle.[141] The lifestyle choices flow out of the relationship.

Though I have presented some evidence indicating that what I'm saying is true, I realize that there is no definitive proof that God exists, and that Jesus is his Son. Believing that requires taking a leap of faith. As the writer of the book of Hebrews stated, "Faith shows the reality of what we hope for; it is the evidence of things we cannot see" (Hebrews 11:1). The one guarantee I can give you is that, if you take this leap of faith, you won't regret it.

In closing, we all have free will. Therefore, each and every one of us is free to choose what we believe. When it comes to choosing what you believe about God and what will happen when you die, I fervently hope and pray that you understand the consequences of your choice.

APPENDIX ONE

For we have heard how the LORD made a dry path for you through the Red Sea when you left Egypt. (Joshua 2:10)

Joshua had to circumcise them because all the men who were old enough to fight in battle when they left Egypt had died in the wilderness. . . . Then the LORD said to Joshua, "Today I have rolled away the shame of your slavery in Egypt." (Joshua 5:4, 9)

Joshua said to the people, "This is what the LORD, the God of Israel, says: Long ago your ancestors, including Terah, the father of Abraham and Nahor, lived beyond the Euphrates River, and they worshiped other gods. But I took your ancestor Abraham from the land beyond the Euphrates and led him into the land of Canaan. I gave him many descendants through his son Isaac. To Isaac I gave Jacob and Esau. To Esau I gave the mountains of Seir, while Jacob and his children went down into Egypt.

Then I sent Moses and Aaron, and I brought terrible plagues on Egypt; and afterward I brought you out as a free people. But when your ancestors arrived at the Red Sea, the Egyptians chased after you with chariots and charioteers. When your ancestors cried out to the LORD, I put darkness between you and the Egyptians. I brought the sea crashing down on the Egyptians, drowning them. With your very own eyes you saw what I did. Then you lived in the wilderness for many years. . . .

The people replied, "We would never abandon the LORD and serve other gods. For the LORD our God is the one who rescued us and our ancestors from slavery in the land of Egypt. He performed mighty miracles before our very eyes. As we traveled through the wilderness among our enemies, he preserved us. (Joshua 24:2–7, 16–17)

The Israelites did evil in the LORD's sight and served the images of Baal. They abandoned the LORD, the God of their ancestors, who had brought them out of Egypt. (Judges 2:11–12)

The LORD sent a prophet to the Israelites. He said, "This is what the LORD, the God of Israel, says: I brought you up out of slavery in Egypt. I rescued you from the Egyptians and from all who oppressed you. I drove out your enemies and gave you their land." . . .

"Sir," Gideon replied, "if the LORD is with us, why has all this happened to us? And where are all the miracles our ancestors told us about? Didn't they say, 'The LORD brought us up out of Egypt'? But now the LORD has abandoned us and handed us over to the Midianites." (Judges 6:8–9, 13)

"Help! Who can save us from these mighty gods of Israel? They are the same gods who destroyed the Egyptians with plagues when Israel was in the wilderness." (1 Samuel 4:8)

"Ever since I brought them from Egypt they have continually abandoned me and followed other gods." (1 Samuel 8:8)

Later Samuel called all the people of Israel to meet before the LORD at Mizpah. And he said, "This is what the LORD, the God of Israel, has declared: I brought you from Egypt and rescued you from the Egyptians and from all of the nations that were oppressing you." (1 Samuel 10:17–18)

"It was the LORD who appointed Moses and Aaron," Samuel continued. "He brought your ancestors out of the land of Egypt. . . .

When the Israelites were in Egypt and cried out to the LORD, he sent Moses and Aaron to rescue them from Egypt and to bring them into this land." (1 Samuel 12:6, 8)

But that same night the LORD said to Nathan,
"Go and tell my servant David, 'This is what the LORD has declared: Are you the one to build a house for me to live in? I have never lived in a house, from the day I brought the Israelites out of Egypt until this very day. I have always moved from one place to another with a tent and a Tabernacle as my dwelling." (2 Samuel 7:4–6)

David's Prayer of Thanks

What other nation on earth is like your people Israel? What other nation, O God, have you redeemed from slavery to be your own people? You made a great name for yourself when you redeemed your people from Egypt. (2 Samuel 7:23)

It was in midspring in the month of Ziv, during the fourth year of Solomon's reign, that he began to construct the Temple of the LORD. This was 480 years after the people of Israel were rescued from their slavery in the land of Egypt. (1 Kings 6:1)

Nothing was in the Ark except the two stone tablets that Moses had placed in it at Mount Sinai, where the LORD made a covenant with the people of Israel when they left the land of Egypt. (1 Kings 8:9)

Then the king turned around to the entire community of Israel standing before him and gave this blessing: "Praise the LORD, the God of Israel, who has kept the promise he made to my father, David. For he told my father, 'From the day I brought my people Israel out of Egypt, I have never chosen a city among any of the tribes of Israel as the place where a Temple should be built to honor my name. But I have chosen David to be king over my people Israel.'" (1 Kings 8:14–16)

This disaster came upon the people of Israel because they worshiped other gods. They sinned against the LORD their God, who had brought them safely out of Egypt and had rescued them from the power of Pharaoh, the king of Egypt. . . .

Worship only the LORD, who brought you out of Egypt with great strength and a powerful arm. Bow down to him alone, and offer sacrifices only to him. (2 Kings 17:7, 36)

"For they have done great evil in my sight and have angered me ever since their ancestors came out of Egypt." (2 Kings 21:15)

"You saw the misery of our ancestors in Egypt, and you heard their cries from beside the Red Sea. You displayed miraculous signs and wonders against Pharaoh, his officials, and all his people, for you knew how arrogantly they were treating our ancestors. You have a glorious reputation that has never been forgotten. You divided the sea for your people so they could walk through on dry land! And then you hurled their enemies into the depths of the sea. They sank like stones beneath the mighty waters. You led our ancestors by a pillar of cloud during the day and a pillar of fire at night so that they could find their way.

You came down at Mount Sinai and spoke to them from heaven. You gave them regulations and instructions that were just, and decrees and commands that were good. You instructed them concerning your holy Sabbath. And you commanded them, through Moses your servant, to obey all your commands, decrees, and instructions.

You gave them bread from heaven when they were hungry and water from the rock when they were thirsty. You commanded them to go and take possession of the land you had sworn to give them." (Nehemiah 9:9–15)

Listen to the word of the LORD, people of Jacob—all you families of Israel! This is what the LORD says:

"What did your ancestors find wrong with me
        that led them to stray so far from me?
They worshiped worthless idols,
        only to become worthless themselves.
They did not ask, 'Where is the LORD
        who brought us safely out of Egypt
and led us through the barren wilderness—
        a land of deserts and pits,
a land of drought and death,
        where no one lives or even travels?'"
(Jeremiah 2:4–6)

"Long ago I broke the yoke that oppressed you
        and tore away the chains of your slavery,
but still you said,
        'I will not serve you.'"
(Jeremiah 2:20)

From the day your ancestors left Egypt until now, I have continued to send my servants, the prophets—day in and day out. (Jeremiah 7:25)

The LORD gave another message to Jeremiah. He said, "Remind the people of Judah and Jerusalem about the terms of my covenant with them. Say to them, 'This is what the LORD, the God of Israel, says: Cursed is anyone who does not obey the terms of my covenant! For I said to your ancestors when I brought them out of the iron-smelting furnace of Egypt, "If you obey me and do whatever I command you, then you will be my people, and I will be your God." I said this so I could keep my promise to your ancestors to give you a land flowing with milk and honey—the land you live in today.'"...

For I solemnly warned your ancestors when I brought them out of Egypt, "Obey me!" I have repeated this warning over and over to this day. (Jeremiah 11:1–5, 7)

"But the time is coming," says the LORD, "when people who are taking an oath will no longer say, 'As surely as the LORD lives, who rescued the people of Israel from the land of Egypt.'" (Jeremiah 16:14)

"The day is coming," says the LORD, "when I will make a new covenant with the people of Israel and Judah. This covenant will not be like the one I made with their ancestors when I took them by the hand and brought them out of the land of Egypt." (Jeremiah 31:31–32)

Jeremiah's Prayer

"You brought Israel out of Egypt with mighty signs and wonders, with a strong hand and powerful arm, and with overwhelming terror. You gave the people of Israel this land that you had promised their ancestors long before—a land flowing with milk and honey." (Jeremiah 32:21–22)

So the Lord gave them this message through Jeremiah: "This is what the LORD, the God of Israel, says: I made a covenant with your ancestors long ago when I rescued them from their slavery in Egypt." (Jeremiah 34:12–13)

Give them this message from the sovereign LORD: When I chose Israel—when I revealed myself to the descendants of Jacob in Egypt—I took a solemn oath that I, the LORD, would be their God. I took a solemn oath that day that I would bring them out of Egypt to a land I had discovered and explored for them—a good land, a land flowing with milk and honey, the best of all lands anywhere. . . .

So I brought them out of Egypt and led them into the wilderness. There I gave them my decrees and regulations so they could find life by keeping them. (Ezekiel 20:5–6, 10–11)

"O Lord our God, you brought lasting honor to your name by rescuing your people from Egypt in a great display of power." (Daniel 9:15)

For I brought you out of Egypt
     and redeemed you from slavery.
     I sent Moses, Aaron, and Miriam to help you.
(Micah 6:4)

Stephen's Sermon Prior to His Stoning

Through the angel who appeared to him in the burning bush, God sent Moses to be their ruler and savior. And by means of many wonders and miraculous signs, he led them out of Egypt, through the Red Sea, and through the wilderness for forty years. (Acts 7:35–36)

Paul's Sermon in Antioch

"The God of this nation of Israel chose our ancestors and made them multiply and grow strong during their stay in Egypt. Then with a powerful arm he led them out of their slavery." (Acts 13:17)

And who was it who rebelled against God, even though they heard his voice? Wasn't it the people Moses led out of Egypt? (Hebrews 3:16)

So I want to remind you, though you already know these things, that Jesus first rescued the nation of Israel from Egypt, but later he destroyed those who did not remain faithful. (Jude 5)

APPENDIX TWO

Then the LORD said to Moses, "I will strike Pharaoh and the land of Egypt with one more blow. After that, Pharaoh will let you leave this country. In fact, he will be so eager to get rid of you that he will force you all to leave." . . .

Moses had announced to Pharaoh, "This is what the LORD says: At midnight tonight I will pass through the heart of Egypt. All the firstborn sons will die in every family in Egypt, from the oldest son of Pharaoh, who sits on his throne, to the oldest son of his lowliest servant girl who grinds the flour. Even the firstborn of all the livestock will die. Then a loud wail will rise throughout the land of Egypt, a wail like no one has heard before or will ever hear again. But among the Israelites it will be so peaceful that not even a dog will bark. Then you will know that the LORD makes a distinction between the Egyptians and the Israelites. All the officials of Egypt will run to me and fall to the ground before me. 'Please leave!' they will beg. 'Hurry! And take all your followers with you.' Only then will I go!" Then, burning with anger, Moses left Pharaoh. (Exodus 11:1, 4–8)

"Announce to the whole community of Israel that on the tenth day of this month each family must choose a lamb or a young goat for a sacrifice, one animal for each household....

"Take special care of this chosen animal until the evening of the fourteenth day of this first month. Then the whole assembly of the community of Israel must slaughter their lamb or young goat at twilight. They are to take some of the blood and smear it on the sides and top of the doorframes of the houses where they eat the animal....

"On that night I will pass through the land of Egypt and strike down every firstborn son and firstborn male animal in the land of Egypt. I will execute judgment against all the gods of Egypt, for I am the Lord! But the blood on your doorposts will serve as a sign, marking the houses where you are staying. When I see the blood, I will pass over you. This plague of death will not touch you when I strike the land of Egypt." ...

So the people of Israel did just as the Lord had commanded through Moses and Aaron. And that night at midnight, the Lord struck down all the firstborn sons in the land of Egypt, from the firstborn son of Pharaoh, who sat on his throne, to the firstborn son of the prisoner in the dungeon. Even the firstborn of their livestock were killed. Pharaoh and all his officials and all the people of Egypt woke up during the night, and loud wailing was heard throughout the land of Egypt. There was not a single house where someone had not died.

Pharaoh sent for Moses and Aaron during the night. "Get out!" he ordered. "Leave my people—and take the rest of the Israelites with you! Go and worship the LORD as you have requested. Take your flocks and herds, as you said, and be gone. Go, but bless me as you leave." All the Egyptians urged the people of Israel to get out of the land as quickly as possible, for they thought, "We will all die!" ...

That night the people of Israel left Rameses and started for Succoth. There were about 600,000 men, plus all the women and children. (Exodus 12:3, 6–7, 12–13, 28–33, 37)

APPENDIX THREE

"That is why I tell you not to worry about everyday life—whether you have enough food and drink, or enough clothes to wear. Isn't life more than food, and your body more than clothing? Look at the birds. They don't plant or harvest or store food in barns, for your heavenly Father feeds them. And aren't you far more valuable to him than they are? Can all your worries add a single moment to your life?

"And why worry about your clothing? Look at the lilies of the field and how they grow. They don't work or make their clothing, yet Solomon in all his glory was not dressed as beautifully as they are. And if God cares so wonderfully for wildflowers that are here today and thrown into the fire tomorrow, he will certainly care for you. Why do you have so little faith?

"So don't worry about these things, saying, 'What will we eat? What will we drink? What will we wear?' These things dominate the thoughts of unbelievers, but your heavenly Father already knows all your needs. Seek the Kingdom of God above all else, and live righteously, and he will give you everything you need." (Matthew 6:25–33)

NOTES

1   Ernest Hemingway, *A Farewell to Arms* (New York, NY: Scribner, 1929), 7.

2   Timothy Keller, *The Reason for God* (New York, NY: Penguin Random House, 2008, 2018), xxiii-xxiv

3   Josh McDowell and Sean McDowell, *Evidence That Demands A Verdict* (Nashville, Tennessee: Thomas Nelson, 2017), xxiii.

4   Timothy Keller, *The Reason for God* (New York, NY: Penguin Random House, 2008, 2018), xxiii.

5   Josh McDowell and Sean McDowell, *Evidence That Demands A Verdict* (Nashville, Tennessee: Thomas Nelson, 2017), xxiii-xxiv.

6   https://hollowverse.com/woody-allen/.

7   Josh McDowell and Sean McDowell, *Evidence That Demands A Verdict* (Nashville, Tennessee: Thomas Nelson, 2017), l.

8   Ibid., li.

9   Timothy Keller, *The Reason for God* (New York, NY: Penguin Random House, 2008, 2018), 75.

10   Ibid., 79.

11   Ibid., 82.

12   Lee Strobel, *The Case for Christ* (Grand Rapids, Michigan: Zondervan, 1998, 2016). 179-80.

13   Timothy Keller, *The Reason for God* (New York, NY: Penguin Random House, 2008, 2018), 84-86.

14   Lee Strobel, *The Case for a Creator* (Grand Rapids, Michigan: Zondervan, 2004), 18-20.

15   Ibid., 27-28

16   Lee Strobel, *The Case for Christ* (Grand Rapids, Michigan: Zondervan, 1998, 2016), 14.

17   Lee Strobel, *The Case for a Creator* (Grand Rapids, Michigan: Zondervan, 2004), 33.

18   Ibid., 37.

19   Ibid., 38.

20   Ibid., 41.

21   Ibid., 43.

22   Ibid., 44-45.

23   Ibid., 49.

24   Ibid., 66.

25   Ibid., 67.

26   Ibid., 69-70.

27   Ibid., 43.

28   Ibid., 44.

29   Ibid., 42.

30   Ibid., 68.

31   Ibid., 69.

32   Ibid., 77.

33   Ibid., 77.

34   Ibid., 80.

35   Ibid., 83.

36   Ibid., 112.

37   Ibid., 114.

38   Ibid., 117.
39   Ibid., 123.
40   Ibid., 130.
41   Ibid., 136-37.
42   Ibid., 143.
43   Ibid., 153.
44   Ibid., 157.
45   Ibid., 158-59.
46   Ibid., 173.
47   Ibid., 197.
48   Ibid., 202.
49   Ibid., 205.
50   Ibid., 222.
51   Ibid., 226.
52   Ibid., 229.
53   Ibid., 232.
54   Ibid., 235-36.
55   Ibid., 238.
56   Ibid., 243-44.
57   Ibid., 251.
58   Ibid., 258.
59   Ibid., 262.
60   Ibid., 278-79.
61   Ibid., 284.
62   Ibid., 292.
63   Ibid., 300-301.
64   Ibid., 302.
65   Ibid., 303.
66   Ibid., 304.
67   Ibid., 86.
68   Ibid., 27.

69   Bruxy Cavey, *The End of Religion* (Colorado Springs, Colorado: NavPress, 2007), 37.

70   Lee Strobel, *The Case for Christ* (Grand Rapids, Michigan: Zondervan, 1998, 2016), 211-12.

71   Ibid., 213-14.

72   Ibid., 214-15.

73   Ibid., 224.

74   Josh McDowell and Sean McDowell, *Evidence That Demands A Verdict* (Nashville, Tennessee: Thomas Nelson, 2017), 237.

75   Ibid., xliv.

76   Eben Alexander, *Proof of Heaven* (New York, NY: Simon and Schuster Paperbacks, 2012), 34-35.

77   Ibid., 8-9.

78   Ibid., 30-31.

79   Ibid., 31-32.

80   Ibid., 38-39.

81   Ibid., 45-47.

82   Ibid., 48.

83   Ibid., 71.

84   Ibid., 69.

85   Ibid., 103-104.

86   Ibid., 147-48.

87   Todd Burpo with Lynn Vincent, *Heaven is for Real* (Nashville, Tennessee: Thomas Nelson, 2010), xvii.

88   Ibid., xviii-xix.

89   Ibid., xix.

90   Ibid., xx-xxi.

91   Ibid., 63.

92   Ibid., 63-64.

93   Ibid., 65, 67.

94   Ibid., 71, 75. 71-75.

95   Ibid., 81.

96   Ibid., 86-87.

97   Ibid., 94-96.

98   Ibid., 100-102.

99   Ibid., 105.

100 Ibid., 107-9.

101 Lee Strobel, *The Case for Christ* (Grand Rapids, Michigan: Zondervan, 1998, 2016), 137.

102 Josh McDowell and Sean McDowell, *Evidence That Demands A Verdict* (Nashville, Tennessee: Thomas Nelson, 2017), 42.

103 Ibid., 46.

104 Ibid., 47.

105 Ibid., 67.

106 Lee Strobel, *The Case for Christ* (Grand Rapids, Michigan: Zondervan, 1998, 2016), 22.

107 Ibid., 23-24.

108 Josh McDowell and Sean McDowell, *Evidence That Demands A Verdict* (Nashville, Tennessee: Thomas Nelson, 2017), 46.

109 Dean G. Miller. *The Wise Men and the Star* (Bloomington, Indiana: WestBow Press, 2019), 99–100.

110 Ibid., 95-97

111 Timothy Keller, *The Reason for God* (New York, NY: Penguin Random House, 2008, 2018), 104.

112 Ibid., 111.

113 Josh McDowell and Sean McDowell, *Evidence That Demands A Verdict* (Nashville, Tennessee: Thomas Nelson, 2017), 91.

114 Ibid., 83.

115 Ibid., 83-84.

116 Ibid., 84.

117 Ibid., 85.

118 Ibid., 86.

119 Ibid., 87.

120 Ibid., 87-88.

121 Lee Strobel, *The Case for Christ* (Grand Rapids, Michigan: Zondervan, 1998, 2016), 90.

122 Josh McDowell and Sean McDowell, *Evidence That Demands A Verdict* (Nashville, Tennessee: Thomas Nelson, 2017), 468.

123 Ibid., 461.

124 Ibid., 474.

125 Ibid., 462.

126 Ibid., 463.

127 Henry T. Blackaby and Claude V. King, *Experiencing God* (Nashville, Tennessee: Thomas Nelson, 2010), 89.

128 Bob Jennerich, *Facing Life's Challenges Head On* (Vellum, 2021). xi-xii.

129 Ibid., xi.

130 Ibid., xii.

131 Ibid., xiii.

132 Ibid.

133 Ibid., 3.

134 John Maxwell, *A Leader's Heart* (Nashville, Tennessee: Thomas Nelson, 2010), 89.

135 Bob Jennerich, *Facing Life's Challenges Head On* (Vellum, 2021), 3, 13-14.

136 Ibid., 14-15.

137 Ibid., 18.

138 Ibid., 17-18.

139 Ibid., 142.

140 Josh McDowell and Sean McDowell, *Evidence That Demands A Verdict* (Nashville, Tennessee: Thomas Nelson, 2017), xxvi.

141 Rick Warren, *The Purpose Driven Life* (Grand Rapids, Michigan: Zondervan, 2002), 18.